Instruction
that measures up

Instruction
that measures up
Successful Teaching in the Age of Accountability

W. James Popham

ASCD

Alexandria, Virginia USA

ASCD®

1703 N. Beauregard St. • Alexandria, VA 22311-1714 USA
Phone: 800-933-2723 or 703-578-9600 • Fax: 703-575-5400
Web site: www.ascd.org • E-mail: member@ascd.org
Author guidelines: www.ascd.org/write

Gene R. Carter, *Executive Director;* Nancy Modrak, *Publisher;* Julie Houtz, *Director of Book Editing & Production;* Katie Martin, *Project Manager;* Cathy Guyer, *Senior Graphic Designer;* Mike Kalyan, *Production Manager;* Keith Demmons, *Desktop Publishing Specialist*

Cartoons by Joan King.

Printed in the United States of America. Cover art © 2009 by ASCD. ASCD publications present a variety of viewpoints. The views expressed or implied in this book should not be interpreted as official positions of the Association.

PAPERBACK ISBN: 978-1-4166-0764-9   ASCD product #108048   n5/09
Also available as an e-book through ebrary, netLibrary, and many online booksellers (see Books in Print for the ISBNs).

Quantity discounts for the paperback edition only: 10–49 copies, 10%; 50+ copies, 15%; for 1,000 or more copies, call 800-933-2723, ext. 5634, or 703-575-5634. For desk copies: member@ascd.org.

Library of Congress Cataloging-in-Publication Data
Popham, W. James.
  Instruction that measures up : successful teaching in the age of accountability / W. James Popham.
      p. cm.
  Includes bibliographical references and index.
  ISBN 978-1-4166-0764-9 (pbk. : alk. paper) 1. Teacher effectiveness. 2. Teachers—Rating of. 3. Effective teaching. 4. Educational accountability. I. Title.

  LB2838.P63 2009
  371.102—dc22
                              2009003693

20 19 18 17 16 15 14 13 12 11 10 09   1 2 3 4 5 6 7 8 9 10 11 12

Instruction
that measures up

Preface

I've spent most of my life in schools of one sort or another. For more than a half-century, I've seen firsthand what goes on in classrooms. Based on those observations, I have no doubt that what's taking place instruction-ally in many of today's classrooms is dramatically different from what was taking place in classrooms when, as a beginning teacher, I cranked out my first lesson plans and used a sometimes-screechy piece of chalk to write my students' assignments on a real slate blackboard.

You could point to countless differences between the classrooms of today and yesterday, including my blackboard's evolution to green (and then to white and completely chalk-free) and the infusion of all sorts of sophisticated electronic gear. But perhaps the most meaningful differ-ence revolves around the use of significant educational tests to provide accountability evidence that schools and teachers are doing what they are supposed to do. That's an enormous change. When I was first teach-ing, if someone at a faculty meeting had used the word *accountability*, my colleagues and I would have thought it referred to what an accoun-tant or a bookkeeper did. Accountability, in those days, had absolutely nothing to do with education. That was then. It's true that the intensity of pressure on teachers to have their students perform well on external accountability tests varies substantially from nation to nation and, within a given nation, from state to state, province to province, and municipality to municipality. But no one in education today could dispute that most of us face a constant pressure to boost students' scores on these critical tests, or that this pressure influences the instruction going on in our classrooms.

Here, then, is the nub of why I decided to tackle the issues addressed in this book. Teachers who are functioning under the scrutiny spawned by today's accountability programs will, understandably, have a response to this palpable evaluative pressure and the way school and teacher success is now dominantly determined by students' test scores. Some teachers aggressively fight accountability programs, in the belief that such initiatives constitute an improper intrusion into their professional domain. Other teachers compliantly accept. Some teachers grudgingly accept but only after gobs of grousing and considerable gnashing of teeth. Still others (and hopefully just a few) attempt to subvert their accountability program by distorting the accuracy of their students' test performances.

I believe the best way for teachers to deal with test-based accountability pressures—*the way that benefits students*—is to accept those pressures as a given, then plan and carry out instruction knowing that it will take place on an accountability-spotlighted stage. What teachers must do is focus on providing instruction that measures up: to the expectations of administrators, parents, and taxpayers; to their own professional standards; and, most essentially, to the needs of their students.

Teaching is, fundamentally, a decision-making endeavor. The most crucial decision teachers make is what to do with the instructional time that's available to them. What will they do? What will they ask their students to do? This book focuses on the kinds of answers a teacher comes up with after taking time to carefully consider the instructional options, and it reflects the reality of making those decisions in this accountability-focused, test-pressured age. Although you will read quite a bit about assessment in the pages to come, this is really a book about instruction and the integral role that assessment plays within the instructional process.

Before we begin, though, I want to engage in some crucial term clarification. When I talk about *assessment*, I'm using the term as a broad descriptor. Assessment includes both traditional paper-and-pencil exams, such as those made up of True/False, short-answer, or multiple-choice items, and a much larger collection of procedures that teachers can use to get a fix on their students' status, including the use of portfolios to document students' evolving skills and the use of anonymous self-report inventories to measure students' attitudes or interests. Assessments also include the variety of informal techniques a teacher might use to check on the status of students' skills for the purpose of guiding instruction rather than for grade-giving, such as when a teacher periodically projects multiple-choice questions on a screen during a lesson and asks students, "on the count of three," to hold up one of four prepared index cards showing the letter of what each student believes is the correct answer.

Speaking of clarification, let's be clear about *teaching*. As educators know, teaching is actually a fairly straightforward undertaking. If you're going to take from this book what I hope you will, you'll recognize that once we strip away its external complexities, teaching boils down to teachers' deciding what they want their students to learn, planning how to promote that learning, implementing those plans, and then determining if the plans worked. I've written this book for teachers and for other educators and school-site administrators who work to improve how teachers teach. If you're a teacher, many of the recommendations I'll offer in the pages to come will be aimed directly at you. If you are an educator who works with teachers, I look to you to be the transmitter of these recommendations.

My fundamental message is that in today's test-pressured educational environment, teachers can make better instructional decisions—the kinds of decisions that benefit students—by deliberately considering the potential relevance of educational testing at critical decision-making junctures during the instructional process. The reality is that the straightforward business of teaching is, in many ways, a test-governed game. We must work to play that game successfully and well, and in a way that makes students come out the winners. This means understanding how assessment can and should influence instruction.

Some writers marry well. They are lucky. Some writers get good editors. They are *really* lucky. On four separate ASCD books, including this one, I have been fortunate to have Katie Martin serve as my editor. I am indebted to her—a collaborator in camouflage.

WJP

May 2009

1

Teaching Through an
Assessment Lens

Given the diverse demands on today's teachers and the complex settings in which those demands must be satisfied, it's easy to lose sight of the fundamental nature of teaching. Teaching exists so that students will learn the things they ought to learn. It's just that simple.

Oh, one could certainly analyze teaching from more sophisticated perspectives. As a teacher-in-training way back when, I studied education from sociological, philosophical, and psychological vantage points. You may have done the same. I read reports from educational sociologists on how society influences a nation's schools and discourse from educational philosophers on how schools affect a society's culture. I read educational psychologists' take on the differences between human learning and sub-human learning. (To this day, I can recall which food-pellet reinforcement schedules are most effective in maintaining a hungry rat's lever-pressing behavior. I keep waiting for an opportunity to use this knowledge.) From these authors, I gained interesting insights on the nuances of schooling. However, such readings did little to allay what, as a prospective teacher, was my all-consuming concern: *What would I actually do when confronted by a classroom of students?* I definitely don't intend to discount the instruction-related contributions of educational philosophers, psychologists, or sociologists, but I'm willing to bet that what most concerns teachers is what most concerned me: the week-to-week, day-to-day, and hour-to-hour instructional decisions to be made.

Teaching as Decision Making

Teachers are obliged to make all sorts of decisions on a continual basis. Some of these decisions meaningfully influence how effectively a teacher teaches; some don't. Classroom management decisions, for example, are almost always an example of the former. If you are a teacher, you might be called on to decide if a handful of students' off-target chatter is significant enough to warrant your intervention. Is this chatter interfering with the learning activities? Is it preventing other students from concentrating? Then, if you decide intervention is warranted, you must decide how to quell such disruptive talking. These decisions clearly will have an effect on how well all the students can learn, including those students doing the off-target chattering. Now, contrast this kind of decision with being asked to decide which of two basically interchangeable computer systems will be installed in your classroom. Your decision between Brand *X* or Brand *Y* computer is apt to have scant impact on the effectiveness of your teaching.

If someone were to analyze every single decision a teacher needs to make during a full school year, many of the most important ones would relate to how students will spend their instructional time—the time devoted to learning what they're supposed to learn. What will the teacher ask students to do in the classroom, for homework, and for longer-term project work and research? What will the students read? What will they listen to? What activities will they engage in, and in what order? These essential decisions about the *means* of instruction proceed from another set of decisions about the *intended outcomes* of that instruction. What is it teachers want their students to learn? Which knowledge and which skills should students master? In other words, once teachers have a fix on what their students are supposed to learn, almost all subsequent decisions will revolve around how those students ought to learn it. Indeed, it is the blend of those two sets of instructional decisions that best characterizes a teacher's general approach to education.

This book about instruction focuses on the most significant decision-occasions teachers face when determining how students should spend their instructional time. As you consider those decision-occasions, I'll urge you to consider instructional methods through the lens of assessment. This is an uncommon way of thinking about teaching, but it's one I advocate strongly, and the reason is simple. In education, the game has changed.

Two Game-Changers in the Instructional Arena

In almost every sphere of human activity, key events or circumstances can alter the ways people behave. We see this in sports, for example, where technical advances in equipment have a major impact on the way a particular game is played. Over the past 10 years, for example, top-level professional tennis has changed from a game of serve-and-volley, in which players serve and then position themselves close to the net, to a game of baseline rallies, with players positioning themselves in the back of the court. Experts attribute this shift in the style of play to advances in tennis racquet design and composition. With newly powerful racquets, players can now strike the ball with enough velocity to easily hit it past an opponent who rushes forward to play close to the net. These high-tech racquets have become, quite literally, game-changers.

For teachers today, two game-changers have emerged in the arena of instruction: (1) the educational accountability movement, built on external accountability tests that purport to measure the effectiveness of instruction, and (2) documentation of the instructional dividends of classroom assessment.

The First Game-Changer: Accountability Tests as the Measure of Teacher Quality

Most accountability tests are administered annually to students at specified grade levels. In many locales, students' performances on these tests are the basis for significant decisions, including whether or not individual test-takers will be promoted to the next grade level or awarded a high school diploma. But, irrespective of a given accountability test's link to rewards or punishments for individual students, it is realistic to regard *all* accountability tests as *high-stakes* assessments. This is because the public regards students' test performances as a way of discerning which educators are doing a good instructional job and which educators aren't. If you teach in a school where students' test scores are the measure of schoolwide success or failure, then the tests involved are—for you— unquestionably high-stakes assessments.

Of course, not all teachers face an annual, score-based appraisal of their personal teaching prowess. Some teachers teach at particular grade levels or in particular content areas where these tests aren't administered. There are no annual accountability tests in fine arts or in physical educa- tion, for example, and accountability tests are far less prevalent in social studies or world languages than they are in mathematics and language arts. But even if you're a teacher whose students *aren't* required to take an accountability test, if you teach in a tax-supported school, odds are that many of your colleagues are currently involved in some sort of account- ability assessments. Moreover, it's almost certain that most are worried about the implications of those assessments.

In many settings, an entire school can be given a label of "failing," or some euphemistic version of that negative descriptor, if even one of the school's demographic subgroups falls below the set performance standard. And the public's confidence in that school as a whole, and in all the school's teachers, will take a hit. Because the success of so many educational professionals is now being determined dominantly by stu- dents' test scores, if you're a teacher, you simply *must* learn about the sorts of assessment instruments being used to distinguish between successful and unsuccessful teachers. Those assessment instruments have an impact on *you*. If you assume a test is a test is a test—that one educational test is pretty much like any other educational test—it's time for an overhaul of your test-related understandings. You'll find the beginnings of such an overhaul in the pages to come.

The Second Game-Changer: The Documented Dividends of Classroom Assessment

More than a decade's worth of research reviews attest to the achievement-boosting payoffs of properly conceived classroom assessments. About 10 years ago, British researchers Paul Black and Dylan Wiliam published a much-cited piece in the *Phi Delta Kappan* (1998b) calling for teachers to employ their classroom assessments in an *instructional manner*. That article was a summary of a previously published, comprehensive review of empirical research focused on whether teachers' use of classroom assessments contributed to students' learning. In that earlier research review, Black and Wiliam (1998a) analyzed more than 680 empirical investigations, first discarding studies they deemed methodologically unsound and then focusing on the results of the remaining 250 well-designed published investigations. Black and Wiliam concluded that student learning improved when the results of classroom assessments were used in a *formatively oriented way*—that is, used to make instructional adjustments either in the way the teacher was teaching something or in the way students were trying to learn something.

Black and Wiliam found that the positive effects of using classroom assessment in this manner were "larger than most of those found for educational interventions" (1998a, p. 61), and this conclusion has been confirmed elsewhere (Crooks, 1988; Shute, 2007; Wiliam, 2007). The fundamental finding in all of these research reviews is that instructionally oriented classroom assessments, if effectively implemented, will improve students' learning (Black, Harrison, Lee, Marshall, & Wiliam, 2004). This led many educators to the rational conclusion that if students' classroom learning improved, then some evidence of this improved learning would show up on their scores on external accountability exams. The emerging body of research indicating well-designed classroom assessments will have a positive impact on students' in-class learning, and—by logical extension—on their scores on accountability exams, is a definite game-changer and the second compelling reason for today's teachers to infuse assessment-thought into almost all aspects of their instructional deliberations.

A Teacher's Must-Make Instructional Decisions

If there were a way to implant a tiny electronic monitoring device inside a willing teacher's skull, we could keep track of all the instruction-related decisions this teacher makes, hour by hour and minute by minute. If we had enough volunteers and implantation devices, as well as a sufficient supply of batteries, we could extend the research and monitor the instructional decisions made by thousands of teachers over an entire school year. And we would find all sorts of decision-making differences among those teachers, attributable to variances in individuals and in the specific instructional settings in which those individuals function. However, it would still be possible to classify their really important instructional decisions into four major categories, each focused on a critical question:

1. *Curricular determination:* Which curricular aims should my students pursue?

2. *Instructional design:* What instructional activities should I provide so my students can achieve the curricular aims I've chosen?

3. *Instructional monitoring:* Do I need to make adjustments in my ongoing instruction and, if so, what sorts of adjustments?

4. *Instructional evaluation:* Were my instructional activities effective and, if not, how should I modify them for future students?

In this book, we will take a close look at each of these critical decisions from both an instructional perspective and an assessment perspective. More specifically, I will ask you to consider the *assessment* considerations that I believe should factor into the *instructional* decisions a teacher needs to make. We'll start now with a little preview, to set the stage.

Decision Set 1: Curriculum Determination

In almost every nation's educational lexicon, the term *curriculum* is sure to be in the Top 10 of teachers' most frequently uttered words. However, if you dig a bit deeper into this particular term-usage, you'd find many different meanings attached to it. And, most certainly, educators' differing interpretations of what *curriculum* actually means often engender confusion. To some, *curriculum* consists of the learning activities taking place in a classroom. To others, the word refers to the instructional materials that teachers use—for instance, the print or electronic materials students are supposed to rely on as they learn. Still other educators use *curriculum* to describe the outcomes teachers try to get their students to attain—for example, the intellectual skills or bodies of knowledge that students are supposed to learn.

In keeping with this book's instructional focus and in support of the cause of clearheadedness, I'd like to set out a single definition of *curriculum* that we'll use for the remainder of the book. It's a definition that I hope will help you think clearly about your own instructional options:

> *Curriculum* describes the outcomes a teacher wishes students to attain.

Most often, those outcomes will consist of *cognitive skills*, such as when students learn to how to solve complex estimation-based word problems in mathematics. Another example of a curricular outcome would be the *bodies of knowledge* students are supposed to acquire, such as a collection of punctuation rules to be used when composing essays or short stories. A curricular outcome might also focus on students' *affect*, for example, when teachers try to get their students to have a more positive attitude toward learning. A curriculum, then, whether it is a national curriculum or the curriculum that *you* choose for your very own students, consists of what it is hoped will be the consequences of instruction. That's right: *Curriculum = Ends*.

So, if curriculum is the ends, it must then follow, as night follows day or as school buses run late, that *Instruction = Means*. At its core, teaching consists of figuring out what *ends* we want students to achieve, and then what *means* we should employ to achieve those ends. The nature of the ends to be promoted instructionally is obviously influential to one's teaching, so teachers need to deal with curricular considerations before they do anything else.

A pause for terminology. Before proceeding further, there are a handful of other curriculum-related terms that could use some clarification. A half-century ago, educators used two descriptors to refer to things they wanted their students to learn: *goals* and *objectives*. A *goal* was a broad, long-term sort of curricular aspiration, one that students might take several months or even a full school year to accomplish. In contrast, an *objective* was a short-term outcome that students might achieve after a few weeks or, possibly, even after a single lesson.

During the last decade or two, educators came to refer to curricular outcomes as *content standards*. It's not clear exactly when this new label was introduced, but it's fairly clear why it became popular. If we educators set out to help our students master challenging outcomes, then we're obviously directing our instruction toward "high standards." And what right-thinking person does not applaud the setting and achieving of high standards? Why, the connotations are almost as heartwarming as those associated with truth, world peace, and fudge brownies!

Typically, but not always, *content standards* describe the broad, long-term outcomes students are supposed to achieve. In a sense, then, most of today's content standards are somewhat akin to yesteryear's goals. However, because lots of content standards are stated in such broad terms that they're difficult to interpret, in many settings we find educators employing a number of other labels to describe the sets of shorter-term, more specific curricular outcomes subsumed under each content standard. So, for example, we encounter *benchmarks, expectancies, indicators,* or other synonymous descriptors that attempt to clarify what achievement of the broad content standard actually entails.

Finally, a number of educators are now using the phrase *curricular aim* to describe an intended outcome of teachers' instructional efforts. I'll use that label in this book for the short-term *or* long-term ends educators have in mind for their students. These ends might be *cognitive, psychomotor,* or *affective*. Cognitive curricular aims, as indicated before, deal with the intellectual skills or bodies of knowledge we want students to learn. Psychomotor curricular aims focus on students' small-muscle skills, such as keyboarding, or large-muscle skills, such as serving a volleyball.

Affective curricular aims describe the attitudes, interests, or values we hope our students will acquire.

Are you, a seasoned educator, required to use the terms that are being trotted out here? Of course not! In real life, you can choose to call the curricular ends that you want your students to accomplish by whatever names you choose ("alligators," "cream puffs"). However, if you're going to get the most out of this book, you'll need to remember I use the term *curriculum* to describe the outcomes (ends) teachers intend to produce in their students as a consequence of their chosen instructional methods (means).

So, for every teacher, the major curricular decision will always focus on answering the following question: *What curricular aims should I pursue for my students?*

This is a deceptively simple question because, as you probably know, and as we'll discuss in Chapter 3, few of today's teachers have total freedom with respect to the curricular ends their students pursue. Most teachers work in environments where governmentally imposed sets of curricular aims exist, and these are the aims teachers are expected to promote with enthusiasm. However, the way that governmentally imposed curricular aspirations are assessed can make a huge difference in the degree to which teachers must toe the curricular line. This is the first place—and quite possibly the most important place—where serious consideration of assessment realities can have a substantial impact on a teacher's instruction.

Decision Set 2: Instructional Design

The second set of instructional decisions a teacher must make focuses explicitly on the means to the chosen curricular ends. If you are a teacher, you need to decide what you will do and what your students will do to attain the curricular aims you (or your school, district, state, or nation) have chosen for these students.

As you'll see when we get to Chapter 4's closer look at instructional design, I believe there is no single, "best way" to teach anything. Students differ substantially in their current achievement levels, their motivations, their personalities, and their previous experiences. These and other variations make a dramatic difference in the most effective way to teach a given group of students. To complicate a teacher's life further, next year's crop of students is likely to be strikingly different from this year's crop of students. Instructional tactics that worked like a whiz last year might flat-out fizzle this year simply because of differences between the two groups of students. Making things even less certain is the obvious fact that teachers differ among themselves in fundamentally important ways. A number of variables—including personality, experience level, understanding of the learning process, understanding of the content, sensitivity to students' confusions, and skill in coming up with lucid explanations—affect how a teacher approaches instruction. So, for any number of reasons, a tactic that works wondrously for one teacher might turn out terribly for another.

On the flip side, two teachers could employ vastly different instructional approaches and still achieve the same desirable outcomes. For me, an event early in my teaching career drove this point emphatically home. A colleague and I were taking turns teaching the same course, switching on a semester-by-semester basis. Although we caucused early on, arriving at a mutually agreed-on set of topics and deciding to use identical final exams, each of us taught the course pretty much as we pleased.

My colleague's teaching style sprang from her belief that students learn best when they are forced to take control of their own learning rather than regard themselves as receptacles for teacher-dispensed truths. Thus, whenever her students asked her a question about the course content, she would invariably respond in a nondirective manner. For example, if John asked her how to approach a particular topic, my colleague would typically respond along these lines: "It's more important, John, what *you* think about how you should approach that topic. What is *your* opinion?"

When my turn to teach the class came, my manner was far more directive. If students asked me a question, I answered immediately and prescriptively. (Back then, I thought I had access to truth, and I wanted to share it. Why withhold "wisdom" from my students?) Where my colleague's teaching style was democratic, mine was borderline fascistic. Yet despite the contrast in our instructional approaches, year after year, there was essentially no difference in how well our students performed on our identical final exams. She had adopted a style that meshed well with who she was. It was the same for me. We had, with respect to teaching, supplied clear confirmatory evidence, albeit anecdotal, for the widely accepted notion there are "different strokes for different folks."

There's a corollary pedagogical reality most seasoned teachers have also discovered: There are no sure-fire, every-time-a-bull's-eye instructional procedures that will always work. Oh, it's true that, as a consequence of thousands of research studies focused on instruction, today's teachers have access to a rather formidable array of teaching techniques that, if employed properly, will *probably* yield positive results. The more conversant you are with today's powerful pedagogical arsenal, the more apt you will be to devise successful instructional designs. Teachers who incorporate research-supported instructional procedures will, even with the enormous variations that exist in teaching situations, be more likely to be effective teachers than will their colleagues who don't use these procedures. But don't be misled. When people refer to a particular instructional technique as *research-proven*, what they mean is that there is empirical evidence the tactic increases the *likelihood* of a successful instructional outcome. There are no instructional techniques that will *always* work with *all* students and *every* teacher for *any* content area in *every* context.

This point is particularly important because, in the teaching game, it's especially easy to fall into an instructional rut that gets gouged more deeply every year. Perhaps because there are so many variables in the classroom, relying on favorite instructional strategies (sometimes irrespective of the degree to which these strategies are effective) can be a tempting constant. Better by far, though, for teachers to concentrate their instructional thinking and decision making on the particular curricular aim they and their students are pursuing. Each teacher must focus on answering this key question: *Do the instructional activities I've designed represent the most effective and efficient way to promote my students' mastery of the curricular aim or aims being sought?*

Decision Set 3: Instructional Monitoring

A teacher's third major arena of instructional decision making revolves around making changes in instructional plans once the instruction is actually underway. Few teachers are naïve enough to believe that a planned set of instructional activities will never need en route modification. Even the most carefully crafted plans can fail to have the desired effect, so instructional flexibility and adjustment are essential to maximize student learning.

For example, suppose you are a 5th grade teacher who has carefully planned a multiweek instructional unit designed to help your students master the curricular aim of persuasive-essay writing. Suppose further that about midway through the unit, your review of students' practice essays shows you that they just aren't getting it. Their essays are emphatically unpersuasive. You immediately recognize that the current slate of instructional activities—what you and your students have done so far and what you have planned for the second half of the unit—simply isn't panning out. Accordingly, you need to adjust what you're doing instructionally . . . but how?

For this third of our major arenas of instructional decision making, every teacher needs to respond to a two-part question: *Do I need to make adjustments in my ongoing instruction and, if so, what sorts of adjustments?* The first half of this two-part question focuses only on whether whatever is going on instructionally needs to be modified *at all*. If there's no need for modification, then the second part of the question instantly evaporates. But if you discover that students aren't learning what you hoped they'd be learning, you must then decide what sorts of changes to make in instruction.

This double-barreled question has a double-barreled answer. Fortunately, during the last decade or so, we have seen a series of research analyses showing that frequent classroom assessment of the appropriate type can provide teachers with the information they need to answer both parts of the question. And, as we'll discuss further in Chapter 5, in addition to supplying teachers with instruction-relevant information, the use of frequent classroom assessments—again, of the appropriate type—can have a powerful positive impact on students' learning. This improved learning not only will be evidenced on teachers' classroom tests but might also show up on externally administered achievement tests, such as today's ubiquitous accountability exams (Black & Wiliam, 1998b; Shute, 2007). One of the most important things teachers who want what's best for their students can do is to continually collect evidence, formally or informally, related to whether they need to adjust their instruction. Chapter 5 will discuss the optimal features and use of classroom assessment.

Decision Set 4: Instructional Evaluation

The fourth and final category of instructional decision making centers on providing an answer to this question: *Did my instruction work?*

This question is short, simple, and absolutely crucial. That's because almost all professionals, teachers included, end up providing the same or similar services again and again over the course of a career. An attorney who specializes in a particular aspect of the law, such as the preparation of wills or the creation of contracts, will prepare wills and craft contracts for years—for different people, of course, but the process is likely to be essentially the same. If such attorneys are competent professionals, they will get better and better at will-generation and contract-crafting as the years go by.

Similarly, teachers teach students, year in and year out, and these teachers' instructional methods focused on particular sets of curricular aims tend to take on a certain constancy. If something works, teachers continue to do it and usually get better and better at doing it. Yes, each year's crop of students is different, which will necessitate some adjustments. Beyond that, the grade level or subject a teacher teaches may change, which will also shake things up. But the true professionals are those teachers who make it their business to discover whether "this year's instruction" was effective and, in so doing, determine if "next year's instruction" needs to be overhauled or merely refined.

Given the reality that students differ all over the lot, and that teachers themselves bring differing instructional expectations to a new school year's teaching, is it certain that this year's *effective* instructional design will be equally effective next year? Of course not. However, probability tells us an instructional design that works well during one school year is *likely* to work fairly well during the next school year. Similarly, an instructional design that proves to be dismal one year, if unchanged for the next year, is *likely* to be similarly dismal the second time around.

For all the variance-related reasons I've mentioned, rarely can anyone look at a planned instructional activity and say for certain that it's going to be effective. In extreme instances, a classroom observer might come up with a pretty solid bet about whether a given instructional sequence is successful or unsuccessful. For instance, if you sat in on a high school history class where the teacher's sole instructional tactic was to have students read paragraphs aloud from their history textbooks, one paragraph per student, chapter after chapter and day after day, you could be pretty confident this instructional approach was a dud. But, most of the time, it's really difficult to focus only on the instructional *process* and accurately appraise how good the instruction really is. This is why we look, instead, at the *consequences* of an instructional design.

To judge the caliber of instructional *means*, we need to find out the nature of the *ends* those means produced. And, as you might have already concluded, here's where assessment has always been seen as having a key role to play. Both educators and non-educators who want to determine whether instruction has been successful now "look at the test scores" to see how instructed students performed. Later, in Chapter 6, I will ask you to consider a variety of ways teachers might evaluate the success of their own instruction, based on students' post-instruction performances. Moreover, in this book you'll be looking at what teachers can do when students' test performances shriek out that instructional changes are in order. Knowing that planned instructional activities have flopped is one thing; figuring out how to remedy a set of sickly instructional activities is something else entirely. There are a number of ways to do precisely that sort of repair job.

A Teacher's Decision-Making Template

Let's pause to see what we've considered in this chapter.

I identified two game-changing factors that have transformed the way teachers need to think about instruction, namely, the arrival of external accountability tests and the documented dividends of suitable classroom assessments. More specifically, I suggested that if today's teachers routinely approach their *instructional* decisions from an *assessment* perspective, then students will be better served. I also identified four kinds of decisions that teachers must invariably address. Those four stages, and the critical question associated with each, are depicted graphically in Figure 1.1.

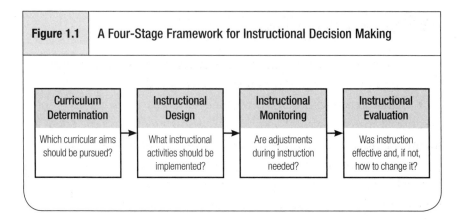

Figure 1.1   A Four-Stage Framework for Instructional Decision Making

Curriculum Determination	Instructional Design	Instructional Monitoring	Instructional Evaluation
Which curricular aims should be pursued?	What instructional activities should be implemented?	Are adjustments during instruction needed?	Was instruction effective and, if not, how to change it?

Although the decisions a teacher makes certainly extend beyond the confines of this four-stage framework, what you see represented in this figure captures the bulk of the instructional choices a teacher will face— at least the really important decisions apt to have an impact on what and how well students learn. Together, these sets of decisions constitute a useful template teachers can routinely employ to consider their chief instructional choices.

Remember, this book about *instruction* is predicated on the conviction a teacher should consider the potential relevance of *assessment* in connection with each of the four clusters of instructional decisions just described. If you are a teacher, know that today—more than ever— students will benefit if you routinely think about the potential impact of assessment at each point in the fourfold framework presented here. The more you understand about the nature of assessment, and particularly about the potential influence of assessment on the instructional decisions you are about to make, the more defensible your resultant decisions will be. Happily, defensible instructional decisions pay off for students.

✔ Chapter Check-Back

- Teaching revolves around the decisions teachers make, the most important of which regard the use of instructional time.
- Classroom teaching has changed over recent years, chiefly because of the educational accountability movement and the documented dividends of instructionally oriented classroom assessments.
- Four sets of decisions encompass the truly crucial choices influencing how well a teacher's students learn: curriculum determination, instructional design, instructional monitoring, and instructional evaluation.
- The four-stage framework for instructional decision making provides a template for thinking about key instructional decisions and for considering the relevance of assessment to each decision.

Suggestions for Further Reading

Black, P., & Wiliam, D. (1998b). Raising standards through classroom assessment. *Phi Delta Kappan, 80*(2), 139–148.

This is a set of school-reform recommendations based on an earlier research review by authors Black and Wiliam. Its publication in a widely circulated U.S. journal attracted considerable attention from American educators to formatively oriented classroom assessment.

Holler, E. W., Gareis, C. R., Martin, J., Clouser, A., & Miller, S. (2008). Teacher-made assessments: Getting them right. *Principal Leadership, 9*(1), 60–64.

Offering practical advice to teachers who construct their own assessments, these middle school educators argue that teacher-made tests must measure skills and knowledge, but at an appropriate level of cognitive engagement.

Popham, W. J. (2001). *The truth about testing: An educator's call to action.* Alexandria, VA: ASCD.

This book attempts to dispel some commonly held misconceptions about educational testing, especially those that bear on a teacher's instructional decisions. Because the book you are currently reading deals with teaching from an unabashed assessment perspective, the more you can learn about instructionally relevant assessment, the better.

Wiliam, D. (2007). Keeping learning on track: Classroom assessment and the regulation of learning. In F. K. Lester, Jr. (Ed.), *Second handbook of mathematics teaching and Learning* (pp. 1053–1098). Greenwich, CT: Information Age Publishing.

This chapter in a book aimed chiefly at mathematics educators updates some of Wiliam's earlier research analysis findings regarding formatively oriented classroom assessments. Although the author's examples are mostly from mathematics, he lays out chief elements of "assessment for learning" in such a way that those elements are readily applicable to all subject areas.

2

A Quick Dip in the Assessment Pool

Before we proceed with an in-depth look at each stage of the assessment-informed, instructional decision-making process, it makes sense to pause for a look at the fundamentals of educational assessment. No, a single chapter will not instantly transform an assessment-oblivious educator into an assessment aficionado, but here you'll find a modest number of concepts, organized into four topic categories, that all educators today must understand if they're going to get maximum instructional mileage out of assessment.

Of course, I don't know if *you*, personally, are well versed in matters related to educational measurement. Many teachers and administrators aren't. If you are familiar with assessment's fundamentals, you may choose to skip this chapter altogether or perhaps just skim through, looking for topics that seem less familiar. Alternatively (or additionally), if you wish to take a longer swim in the assessment pool, this chapter's Suggestions for Further Reading (see p. 51) will point you toward sources that address many of these topics in greater detail. For those who wish to accompany me on this terse tour of assessment's bread-and-butter basics, let's begin with "Topic 1": the reason we test students in the first place.

Testing as Score-Based Inference Making

We teach students so that they will learn the things we want them to learn, and we test them because it's a way to figure out what level of "thing learning" students have attained. Tests provide a way around the simple truth that a student's knowledge, cognitive skills, and affect are *covert*. It's impossible to tell how skilled a speller Jerome is simply by looking at Jerome. His reading abilities and his knowledge of world history are similarly covert. Of course, Jerome's teachers want to make him a better speller, a great reader, and a world-history wizard. How can they tell if he's progressing satisfactorily toward the curricular aims they've set for him?

That's right: They test him.

Teachers provide opportunities for students to display skills or knowledge *overtly* by having them take a test. Then, based on students' overt test performances, they can arrive at an *inference* regarding those students' unobservable skills and knowledge. So, Jerome's language arts teacher, Ms. Berry, might administer a dictation-style spelling test consisting of 20 tough-to-spell words, reading each word out loud and asking Jerome and his classmates to write the proper spelling of each word in their test booklets. Depending on how well Jerome does on this test, Ms. Berry can *infer* whether Jerome is a super speller (20 items correct), a shoddy speller (3 items correct), or somewhere in between.

Without this test-based form of inference making, teachers couldn't reach any sensible conclusions regarding their students' levels of achievement. Figuring out how students were learning would be guesswork. Typically, we describe this central role of educational assessment by saying educators arrive at estimates of students' abilities via *score-based inferences* or, if you prefer, via *test-based inferences*. In its most basic form, educational assessment is an inference-making enterprise wherein educators look at students' test scores and interpret the meaning of those scores: What levels of knowledge or mastery do students' scores represent? What do those test scores signify about those students?

The reason it's important to stress that testing is fundamentally an inference-making endeavor is because inferences are made by *people*, and people are far from infallible. Tests—the instruments we use to obtain students' scores—do not, all by themselves, furnish the necessary inferences; it's teachers who do the inference making, who decide what the meaning of a student's test score is. To do that well, teachers need to be able to examine the suitability of a test and determine if it is, in fact, a sound foundation for inference making. And this is why every teacher must be familiar with at least the basics of educational assessment.

The Core Concepts of Assessment

Traditionally, the most fundamental concepts associated with educational assessment are *reliability*, *validity*, and *bias*. The Era of Accountability Testing has introduced a fourth concept: the notion of a test's *instructional sensitivity* as a key consideration in judging that test's suitability for a particular use. Over the next few pages, you'll encounter the requisite dollops of information you need regarding each of these concepts. Let's get to it.

Core Concept 1: Reliability

Assessment *reliability* refers to the consistency with which a test measures whatever it's measuring. Sounds simple enough. In fact, if you remember that *reliability* = *consistency*, you've mastered most of what you need to know about assessment reliability.

What can be a little confusing is that there are three strikingly different ways to characterize a test's consistency. For reasons I'll explain shortly, it's important to be aware of these differences and not assume that all statements about a test's reliability are referring to the same thing.

Stability reliability. A test's *stability reliability* refers to the test's consistency of measurement on different occasions. Suppose a teacher gave her students a test on May 1, administered the same test to the same students again on May 15 (without providing additional instruction in the intervening weeks), and then compared individual students' scores on the two testing occasions. If the test possesses stability reliability, the scores will be similar. For obvious reasons, this kind of reliability is sometimes referred to as *test-retest reliability*.

What's taking place when a test fails to yield consistent scores on two time-separated occasions? Often it's a case of the test containing a number of ambiguous and confusing items. If kids can't figure out what a question is really asking, there's a good chance they will answer one way on one testing occasion and a different way on a subsequent occasion. Another explanation for low stability reliability is the presence of lots of items dealing with content that's outside what has been emphasized instructionally. For example, on a 7th grade history test, the teacher might have included several multiple-choice items dealing with historical details that, though interesting to the teacher, were never covered in class or in students' assigned reading. When presented with such items, almost all students will be obliged to do some serious guessing. Again, truly knowledgeable kids, that is, the ones who mastered what they were actually taught, might answer correctly on one testing occasion and incorrectly on a second testing occasion. Unknowledgeable students might similarly flip-flop on such items between two separate testing occasions. For a test to have high stability reliability, test developers need to construct scads of items that the most knowledgeable students will answer correctly whenever they're tested and the least knowledgeable students will stumble over whenever they are tested.

A test's stability reliability can be represented in two ways. The first is through a *correlation-based approach*, which requires the computation of a *correlation coefficient*, a numerical index representing the strength and direction of the relationship between the same students' scores on two testing occasions. A test's correlation coefficient (symbolized in "test talk" and documentation as r) can range from -1.00 to $+1.00$, with a coefficient of 0 (zero) signifying no relationship at all between students' scores on the two testing occasions. A strong positive correlation coefficient indicates that students' scores on the two occasions were similar. An r of 1.00, for example, would signify that all students' performances were ranked identically for the two tests—that is, Millie scored highest on both tests, Billy scored second highest on both tests, and so on. Depending on the nature and length of the test itself, and the duration of the delay between the two testing occasions, measurement specialists hope to see positive stability coefficients in the neighborhood of $r =$ .70 or higher. For longer, well-constructed tests and for tests with short between-test intervals, stability coefficients are often considerably higher, perhaps around .90 or so.

The second way of representing a test's stability reliability is to calculate the *decision consistency* of the test between the two test-administrations. These days, test scores are often used to classify students into categories. For example, test scores on a 60-item, district-developed mathematics exam might be used to determine which students will be enrolled in a remedial summer math program. If the decision is that students who miss 20 or more items will be enrolled in the program, then students who score 40 and below would be placed into one category ("summer program required"), while students who score 41 or above would be placed in a second category ("summer program not required").

Calculating a test's stability using a decision-consistency procedure entails determining the percent of students who are classified identically on the two testing occasions. Thus, if 92 percent of the students were classified the same way based on the two test-administrations—that is, if adding the percent of students who were required to take the summer program (based on both test-administrations) to the percent of students who were not required to do so (based on both test-administrations) turned out to be 92 percent—then the test would be said to have a stability reliability estimate of 92 percent. The idea is that, irrespective of whether a student scored 48 on the first test-administration and 59 on the second test-administration, the scores are similar enough in the more-than-40-items-correct category so that the same *decision* would be made about that student ("no summer math program required").

Historically, a test's reliability has been represented by using correlation coefficients, but recently we have seen more and more reliance on the use of decision-consistency estimates when test reliability is reported in technical manuals. This is chiefly because decision-consistency estimates make more intuitive sense. Parents, educators, and lay citizens can understand what it means if it is reported that "when this test was used on two time-separated occasions, test-takers were classified into identical categories 93 percent of the time." Nonetheless, educators should be prepared to encounter estimates of a test's reliability based on either correlation-based or decision-consistency approaches.

Alternate-form reliability. The name of *alternate-form reliability* offers a solid clue to what it is: the degree to which two different versions (or "forms") of a test are consistently measuring whatever they're intended to measure. With today's increasingly widespread use of tests to make important decisions about students, it is fairly common to encounter two or more forms of a test designed to measure the same thing. Multiple forms of a test are often needed when a student must re-take a given test and those administering the test do not want the test-taker's earlier exposure to that test to skew the retake score.

All that's done to determine the alternate-form reliability of two test forms is to administer each form to the same students, with little or no delay, and then analyze the results using either a correlational or a decision-consistency approach. There are no magic "good enough" minimum numbers that tests must attain before they are thought to possess acceptable alternate-form reliability, but high levels of consistency between the two forms are obviously desirable.

Internal consistency reliability. In contrast to the previous two types of reliability, *internal consistency reliability* requires only a single test-administration to a single group of students. This is because it represents the degree to which a test's *items* appear to be doing the same consistent measurement job. Internal consistency coefficients are based on intercorrelations among a test's items, and higher internal consistency r-values indicate a test's items are functioning homogeneously and measuring the same thing in pretty much the same way.

Because calculating this type of reliability evidence requires just a single test-administration, internal consistency reliability tends to be computed far more frequently than either stability or alternate-form reliability coefficients. Note that because there are no student-classification decisions directly linked to this form of reliability, only correlational approaches are used to determine a test's internal consistency. With most large-scale standardized achievement tests, internal consistency estimates often reach reliability coefficients of .90 or higher.

Assessment consistency for *students* versus assessment consistency for *a student*. The three kinds of reliability we've looked at all focus on assessment consistency in terms of *groups* of students rather than *one* student. To get a fix on how reliable a test is when it is used for one student at a time, psychometricians have come up with an index called the *standard error of measurement* (SEM), which is intended to indicate how likely it is that the same student, taking the same test on different occasions or taking two different forms of the same test, will get consistent scores on those tests. The SEM is similar to the error margins often presented along with opinion polls where, for example, results with a ±3 percent error margin are regarded as more accurate than results accompanied by a ±10 percent error margin. The larger a test's standard error of measurement is, the less reliable that test will be when used to measure a particular student. The smaller a standard error of measurement is, the more reliable the test will be when assessing any one student. Repeating: A smaller SEM is good; a larger SEM is the opposite.

This is the perfect time to point out that teachers must recognize educational assessment devices for what they are: measurement tools that are far from flawless. It serves no one to ascribe unwarranted precision to educational tests. It's true that test scores are numbers, and sometimes even numbers containing impressively precise decimal points, but they nonetheless represent *approximations*, not sanctified truths. Remember, even measurement experts refer to a *standard* error of measurement, and that's no accident. Errors of measurement are so pervasive that they most certainly are standard.

About now, you may be asking yourself, *how does this discussion of reliability relate to me?* If you're a teacher, is it really important that you learn how to compute reliability indices for the classroom tests you make? No, it isn't. Realistically, few classroom teachers have the time to compute reliability indices of any sort for their own tests. Even most psychometricians, people who really revel in computing reliability indices for large-scale tests, would privately concede that it is not cost-effective for classroom teachers to spend their instructional planning time computing reliability estimates for their tests.

However, it *is* extremely important for all educators to recognize that the three types of reliability evidence a test may tout are fundamentally different. For instance, if a standardized test is accompanied by glistening evidence of the test's internal consistency reliability, you should not assume that this evidence will automatically translate into high stability reliability for the test. It won't. Such a test may be chock-a-block full of items measuring the same stuff, which makes it internally consistent, but if re-administered one month later to the same students, it might yield rather inconsistent scores. Don't assume that just because a test sports an impressive internal consistency r-value, this tells you anything about the test's alternate-form consistency and whether Test Form A and Test Form B will be measuring students similarly. It doesn't. The three types of reliability are different: separate pictures of how consistently a test measures what it's supposed to measure and, thus, how useful it will be to teachers as they carry out the critical work of score-based inference making.

Core Concept 2: Validity

The second of the core concepts of educational measurement is rooted even more firmly in the making of test-based inferences. Essentially, *validity* = *inference accuracy*. The term *valid* does not refer to an attribute of tests themselves but, rather, to the accuracy of test-based inferences individuals make based on the test's results. So, even though we often hear people talking about "a valid test," this is technically incorrect. It's not a test that's valid or invalid; it's the score-based inference we make about the test results that's valid or invalid.

It is an educator's job to arrive at a correct interpretation of students' test scores, and anyone who believes accuracy is somehow resident in a test itself might be too inclined to acquiesce to the "valid" test's results. What educators ought to be focusing on and judging is the accuracy of test-based *inferences* they make. The first step in that process is remembering there is no such thing as "a valid test."

Just as there are three varieties of evidence bearing on the reliability of a test, there are also three types of evidence related to the validity of test-based inferences. (What can I say? Psychometricians apparently groove on threes.) We'll take a peek at all three of these types of validity evidence just so you'll know what they are, but I'll start with—and give most of the attention to—the type of validity evidence most relevant to classroom teachers.

Content-related evidence of validity. This form of validity evidence describes the extent to which a test appears to adequately represent the content of the curricular aim or aims that the test is supposed to measure.

Tests, as we know, almost always *sample* the various skills and bodies of knowledge embodied in a curricular aim. If you were a teacher putting together a mathematics test to see if your students are skilled in multiplying pairs of triple-digit numbers, you'd probably give them a handful of these triple-digit numbers to multiply. One such item on the test might be this: $142 \times 387 = ?$

Yes, there are oodles of triple-digit number combinations that would be eligible to assess a student's triple-digit multiplication skill, but to assess students using *all* possible combinations of triple-digit numbers would be absurd. So, on practicality grounds, you would typically draw a *sample* from all possible triple-digit number combinations, then base your inference about a student's triple-digit multiplication skill on the student's ability to deal with that sample of multiplication problems.

Content-related evidence of validity focuses on whether the test's sample is *sufficiently representative* of whatever set of skills or knowledge it is attempting to sample. To illustrate this kind of evidence, think back to the beginning of this chapter and the 20-item spelling test that Ms. Berry administered to Jerome and her other students. Are the 20 tough-to-spell words Ms. Berry selected for her test enough words to give her an accurate picture of her students' covert spelling ability? Are they the right kinds of words, representative of the letter combinations and vowel blends likely to trip up a less-than-stellar speller? Clearly, the more adequately a test represents the content embodied in a curricular aim, the more valid will be any test-based inference regarding students' mastery of the curricular aim that's assessed.

The broader the scope of a curricular aim, the more difficult it is to represent that aim satisfactorily via a sample-based test. Small-scope curricular aims, such as mastery of triple-digit multiplication, are far easier to represent, even with a short test, than are broad-scope curricular aims, such as a student's ability to solve multiple-operation, multiple-step mathematics word problems. Similarly, if a history test is supposed to measure a student's ability to apply a full century's worth of historical lessons to a wide range of current-day social problems, then content representation is much more challenging than when historical lessons from one event are applied to one current-day problem.

While evidence of test reliability is *calculated,* evidence of test validity is *gathered,* as it is almost always based on teachers' and other education professionals' judgment of how well the test represents a curricular aim's content. The more systematically those judgments have been gathered, the stronger the resultant content-related evidence of validity will be. When test-making firms need content-related validity evidence for important educational tests, they take great care to assemble large groups of teachers who render a series of carefully structured judgments about a test's individual items as well as its overall content representativeness.

For busy teachers, less elaborate scrutiny of classroom tests is the norm. However, a teacher who tries to design tests that truly represent the full range of content present in whatever curricular aims those tests are meant to assess can have greater confidence in any subsequent, test-based inference about students' achievement levels. For this reason, I recommend all teachers who construct their own classroom assessments consider collecting content-related evidence of those tests' validity. One straightforward way to collect content-related evidence for a teacher-made test is to first focus on *items,* then deal with the content representativeness of the curricular *aim* (or *aims*) being assessed. Regarding items, a teacher can ask the following question about each item on the test.[1]

---

[1] To simplify this example, I am going to assume that this test assesses only one curricular aim, but the same approach will work with a multi-aim test, taken one aim at a time.

A per-item content question: *Will a student's response to this item, along with other items, contribute to a valid inference regarding the student's mastery of the curricular aim being assessed?* (Responses might be Yes, No, or Uncertain.)

Then, after responding to this question for each item in the test and, thereafter, documenting the percent of items that were judged to contribute to a valid inference about students' curricular aim mastery, the teacher's attention turns to the curricular aim being assessed.

A curricular aim representation question: *After thinking carefully about the complete range of content embodied in the curricular aim being assessed, what percent of that content has been adequately assessed by the total set of items in this test?* (Responses might be in 10 percent increments, for instance, 70 percent or 90 percent, depending on the teacher's judgment.)

Clearly, what the teacher would like to see when collecting this sort of content-validity evidence is (for question 1) a high proportion of items judged to contribute to a valid inference about a student's mastery status and (for question 2) a high percentage number—thereby indicating satisfactory content representation by the test.

By carrying out this sort of evidence-collection process and documenting it for their most important tests, teachers will find that the content representativeness of their key classroom tests will be substantially strengthened.

Criterion-related evidence of validity. The second of our three kinds of validity evidence is applicable whenever a test is employed to predict how well test-takers will perform in some subsequent situation—typically in a future academic setting. To illustrate, when high school students are asked to complete a college entrance exam such as the SAT or ACT, those students' test performances are supposed to be predictive of the students' subsequent grades in college. In this situation, college grades are the *criterion*. Thus, we see that students' scores on a predictor test (the college entrance exam) are supposed to accurately forecast those students' subsequent performances with respect to the criterion (the college grades).

Criterion-related evidence of validity is collected by determining how accurate a set of test-based predictions actually is. Typically, this involves computing a correlation coefficient between students' predictor-test scores (say, on the SAT) and those same students' criterion scores (their subsequent college grade-point averages). In the case of most college entrance exams, the correlation between students' test scores and their college grade-point averages turns out to be approximately .50.

What does a college entrance exam's correlation coefficient of .50 mean? A layperson might look at it and conclude, erroneously, that a high SAT score accurately predicts college grades about 50 percent of the time. But psychometricians know that to determine the predictive usefulness of a correlation coefficient, you must *square* it. If we multiply the correlation coefficient of .50 by itself, we get a new number: .25. What this .25 signifies is that students' scores on college admissions exams (the predictor test) might be expected to accurately account for about 25 percent of students' college grades (the criterion). Yes, although college entrance exams are touted as accurate predictors of the grades students will earn in college, this is simply not so. Fully 75 percent of college grades are accounted for by *non-test* factors, such as a student's study habits and, in particular, a student's level of effort.

Construct-related evidence of validity. The final member of our validity evidence trio is difficult to describe in a short-and-sweet way. Technically, *construct-related evidence* of validity describes the extent to which empirical evidence—that is, evidence verifiable by experience or experiment—confirms the existence of an inferred hypothetical construct and demonstrates a given exam's ability to accurately assess an examinee's status with respect to the inferred construct.

Here's a less high-brow way of putting it: Because we can't see inside students' heads, we must infer what's going on in there. We might, for instance, infer that a student chess player who repeatedly wins matches against much older opponents possesses good "chess-playing ability." In this case, "chess-playing ability" is an inferred, hypothetical construct. It represents the way we've decided to depict the unseeable ability levels of persons who play chess. Similarly, if we refer to a student as being an excellent reader, someone whose "reading comprehension" is outstanding, "reading comprehension" is the inferred, hypothetical construct. Educators employ inferred constructs all the time because hypothetical constructs are useful.

When collecting construct-related evidence of a test's validity, we must assemble empirical evidence, such as students' pre-test and post-test scores, to see not only if such evidence confirms that the hypothetical construct we've inferred is a reasonable one (for example, "reading comprehension" is something that exists), but also whether or not the test we're evaluating seems to be properly measuring test-takers' status with respect to that inferred construct. These sorts of construct validation studies can get super-sticky—and quite quickly, and they don't have tons of practical applications for classroom teachers. If you're a budding psychometrician, however, there's been plenty written about construct-related evidence of validity that you may find fascinating. As with all of the other assessment-focused topics in this chapter, you can learn much more about this and all kinds of validity by consulting the Suggestions for Further Reading references on page 51.

Core Concept 3: Assessment Bias

For too many years, numerous educational tests were unarguably biased against certain groups of students in a way that negatively affected those students' scores and, consequently, supported unsound inferences about those students' aptitude and achievement levels. Fortunately, during the past few decades, large-scale test-makers have become far more attentive to the eradication of bias in their assessment instruments.

Assessment bias refers to qualities of an assessment that offend or unfairly penalize a group of students because of gender, race, ethnicity, socioeconomic status (SES), religion, or other group-defining characteristic. Tests can be *offensive* to test-takers whenever negative stereotypes of certain subgroup members are present in a test's items. If a student who is a member of a negatively test-depicted subgroup becomes upset by such a depiction (for instance, by an insensitively worded test item), the student's performance on subsequent test items is often adversely affected. Similarly, students can experience *unfair penalties* when a test includes content that's likely to be familiar to students in some subgroups but not to students outside these subgroups. So, for instance, if a language arts achievement test contains test items incorporating cultural content that's apt to be better known to native-born students than to students who are recent immigrants, this would be a clear instance of unfair penalization.

When judging the presence of assessment bias in large-scale accountability tests, it is common to assemble a *bias-review panel* consisting of educators representing those subgroups who have historically been on the receiving end of assessment bias in that locale. Then the bias-review panelists go through the test item by item, rendering judgments in response to a question such as this one: *Might this item offend or unfairly penalize any group of students on the basis of personal characteristics such as gender, ethnicity, or religion?*

If you're a teacher who wants to detect and eliminate assessment bias in your own tests, engaging in a more informal application of this kind of per-item bias question will almost always prove helpful. Any such potential bias, if located, should be summarily expunged.

Core Concept 4: Instructional Sensitivity

The final of the four fundamentals of assessment that educators should know about is especially important in these accountability-driven times, and it's one that only recently has become of concern to members of the educational measurement community. I am referring to a test's *instructional sensitivity*: the degree to which students' performances on that test accurately reflect the quality of instruction specifically provided to those students for the purpose of promoting their mastery of the content being assessed.

Instructional sensitivity is a critical consideration whenever tests are being employed as part of a program to evaluate schools or, more accurately, to evaluate those educators who staff a school. When students' test scores are the basis of educational accountability, those test scores must accurately reflect the caliber of instruction students receive. If these tests are instructionally *insensitive*, the underlying premise of test-based accountability programs collapses. Instruction may be good, poor, or improving, but students' test scores won't show it.

Before dealing with *why* an accountability test is instructionally sensitive or insensitive, let's be sure we're clear about what's going on in those two kinds of tests. We can start by looking at an instructionally *sensitive* test, and by assuming that a teacher has been assigned essentially the same sorts of students year after year. (Yes, this is unlikely, but in Assumption Land, we're allowed to make things a skosh simpler for the purposes of explanation.) Well, if our imaginary teacher's instruction gets better every year, then students' scores on each year's instructionally sensitive accountability test will likewise be higher every year. If the teacher's instruction doesn't improve or declines in quality, then students' scores on that instructionally sensitive test won't get higher or will drop . . . and the teacher and school will be held accountable. This is, without question, the way a test-based educational accountability system ought to function.

Let's turn, now, to an instructionally *insensitive* test. With such a test, our imaginary teacher's instruction could improve year after year, but there will be no corresponding rise in students' test scores. Strong instruction simply won't show up when students take an instructionally insensitive test. Neither will weak instruction; if our teacher's instruction stagnates or declines in quality, students' test scores won't reflect that, either. Simply put, instructionally insensitive tests mask the quality of teaching.

Now, to be realistic, it makes more sense to think about a test's instructional sensitivity in the form of a 10-point "continuum of sensitivity" rather than as an on/off quality. Tests can range dramatically on the degree of instructional sensitivity they embody. Still, few educators, though seemingly awash in an ocean of test-based accountability, currently recognize how few accountability tests are even mildly sensitive to the caliber of a teacher's instruction.

What makes a test instructionally insensitive? The two major factors underlying a test's instructional insensitivity are associated with the way the test has been constructed and the number of curricular aims it attempts to assess. Let's look briefly at each factor.

Faulty construction. The standardized achievement test—that is, a test administered, scored, and interpreted in a standard, predetermined manner—is the poster child for tests that are inherently instructionally insensitive by virtue of their design. For nearly a century, standardized achievement tests have been constructed with a specific measurement mission: to arrive at *comparative interpretations* of test-takers' scores. What this means, typically, is that a student's score is compared and contrasted with the scores of previous students, who are referred to as the test's *norm group.* This is how we learn, for example, that Barbara's score is at the 96th percentile in relation to scores of norm-group students, while Caitlyn's score is at the 35th percentile. The complication is that to arrive at such comparisons efficiently, it is imperative that the test produces a substantial amount of *score-spread.* In other words, test-takers' scores need to be scattered over a wide range of possible score-points. One of the most statistically efficient ways to increase a test's score-spread is to include items test-makers believe roughly half of test-takers will answer correctly. And if we look at the sorts of items these turn out to be, that's when our instructional-sensitivity plot begins to thicken.

Because the socioeconomic status of students' families is a nicely spread-out variable, and a variable that isn't altered very rapidly, test items including content likely to be familiar to students from high-SES families but not to students from low-SES families do a terrific job in producing score-spread. Items linked to inherited academic aptitudes are similarly effective, as there are substantial differences among students when it comes to in-born verbal, quantitative, and spatial aptitudes. Students who drew higher levels of these academic aptitudes in the gene-pool lottery tend to score better on aptitude-linked items than their classmates who drew lower levels. The purpose of this kind of test construction is not malicious so much as it is practical: These items do a crackerjack job of producing the score-spread that is indispensable if standardized achievement tests are to fulfill their comparative score-interpretation mission.

Many of today's educational accountability tests have been constructed using these same sorts of traditional test-development procedures, focused on *comparative* score interpretations. Yet, because numerous score-spreading items on such tests are linked to students' SES or to students' inherited academic aptitudes, these tests tend to measure what students *bring* to school rather than what students have been taught once they arrive at school.

Too many curricular aims. Most of today's standards-based accountability tests serve as perfect examples of the second sort of instructionally insensitive tests. These tests, ostensibly built so educators can determine whether students are mastering collections of official content standards, represent a sensible approach to accountability testing, at least in theory. That theory goes like this: A set of intended curricular outcomes (the content standards) will first be isolated, then tests will be constructed to determine if students have achieved those intended curricular outcomes. This makes a sackful of sense. But something went wrong in the implementation of this reasonable test-based approach to educational accountability, and most of today's standards-based accountability tests have turned out to be instructionally insensitive.

The reason? Well, when most sets of official, to-be-assessed curricular aims are actually chosen, the choosers opt for far too many aims. Those subject-matter specialists who identify official content standards for a given subject area more often than not identify *all* the skills and knowledge they *wish* students would master rather than put together sets of realistic curricular expectations. In some settings, teachers are asked to promote their students' mastery of several hundred curricular aims. Given the teaching time available, it's a task that's patently impossible from an instructional perspective. And it's every bit as impossible from an assessment perspective.

If there are too many curricular aims to be assessed on a standards-based accountability test, the test's developers have no choice but to measure only a sample of these aims. Some curricular aims will be assessed annually, some will be assessed only in certain years, and some won't *ever* be assessed. Given such circumstances, teachers who are trying to get their students ready for an annual accountability test must *guess* about which of the eligible curricular aims will actually show up on that year's test, then focus their instruction on those aims. Inevitably, many teachers guess wrong.

After a few years of mistaken guessing, there are teachers who will simply abandon their fruitless efforts to teach all the official content standards and prepare students for unpredictable tests alleged to assess students' mastery of those content standards. At that point, guess which factors step in to contribute most heavily to students' scores on these standards-based accountability tests? Yes, it turns out to be students'

SES and their inherited academic aptitudes—the same two variables so dominant in determining students' scores on standardized achievement tests. Thus, good intentions notwithstanding, many standards-based accountability tests also tend to measure what students bring to school rather than what students learn in the classroom.

What makes a test instructionally sensitive? An accountability test that's instructionally sensitive has four indispensable attributes.

It assesses only a modest number of super-significant curricular aims. To help ensure that the number of curricular aims to be measured can be taught in the available instructional time and assessed in the available testing time, the number of curricular aims an accountability test covers should be in the 5 to 10 range rather than the 50 to 100 range. Each of the curricular aims tested, however, should be a remarkably significant educational outcome, subsuming a host of important subskills and bodies of enabling knowledge.

It is accompanied by a detailed description of each assessed curricular aim so that teachers can accurately target their instruction. The essence of each curricular aim to be assessed must be described in relatively brief, teacher-palatable language so teachers can direct their instruction toward the curricular aim itself rather than toward specific test items measuring that aim. A page or two of plain-talk descriptive information, typically accompanied by a few illustrative items, can provide teachers with a sufficiently clear understanding of what's to be tested and, hence, what's to be taught.

It provides per-curricular-aim reporting for every student. Limiting the pool of curricular aims to be assessed makes it feasible to include several items for each of those curricular aims. This means it's possible to generate sufficient data to capture the test-taker's status in relation to each curricular aim, and an instructionally sensitive test communicates this information in individual student reports. These reports should be transmitted to teachers, students, and students' parents. Because teachers can aggregate their own students' per-aim performances, they can then determine the success of their own instruction related to each curricular aim.

Its items have been screened for instructional sensitivity. The final measure of a test's instructional sensitivity is the degree to which each of its items is sensitive to instructional impact. Per-item judgments can be made about whether each item is (1) free from dominant SES influence, (2) free from dominant inherited academic aptitude influence, and (3) responsive to instruction, which is another way of saying the extent to which the person reviewing the item believes that most well-taught students would be likely to answer it correctly.

In Mississippi and Wyoming, state education officials are undertaking additional experimental efforts to collect empirical evidence of the instructional sensitivity of accountability test items. Teachers in these states submit signed questionnaires identifying the curricular aims that they have taught with the most and the least instructional success, relatively speaking. Next, their students' accountability tests are analyzed to contrast per-item performances on "successfully taught" and "unsuccessfully taught" curricular aims. Items that fail to distinguish between successfully and unsuccessfully taught curricular aims are then reviewed for possible deletion from those states' accountability tests.

If these four attributes are incorporated into the test's design from the outset, it is possible to build an instructionally sensitive accountability test—one that can provide accurate evidence of school quality and serve as a catalyst for instructional improvement in the classroom. Because few of today's accountability tests were actually built to be instructionally sensitive, it's not surprising that most of them are not.

What teachers need to recognize is that the degree to which the accountability tests in their setting are (or aren't) instructionally sensitive should have a giant impact on many of those teachers' instructional decisions, and in later chapters, we'll go into the particulars. Although the instructional sensitivity of an accountability test is important any time that the results are used to evaluate instructional quality, the instructional sensitivity of classroom tests matters to any teacher who is looking for evidence of his or her own instructional effectiveness.

The Categories of Educational Tests

It is said that there are many ways to cut a cake—something my own experience with cake cutting confirms to be true. Similarly, when looking at the entire array of educational assessments that an educator might encounter, there are diverse slicing strategies available to subdivide "assessments" into constituent chunks. Let's briefly identify some of the chief, instructionally relevant genres of educational assessments. All of the kinds of tests I'll be describing have direct implications for a teacher's instructional decisions.

Aptitude Tests and Achievement Tests

Historically, there has been a distinction drawn between educational *aptitude* tests and educational *achievement* tests. Whereas aptitude tests were thought to measure a student's potential, according to aptitudes usually believed to be genetically inherited, achievement tests were presumed to measure what a student had learned—typically the sorts of knowledge and skills that have been taught in school. In recent years, aptitude tests have been increasingly criticized on the grounds that they are not only too genetically dependent but also insufficiently predictive. As we've already noted, although students' scores on the widely used SAT college admission test are predictive of the grades a student subsequently earns in college, the precision of those predictions leaves much to be desired.

Even so, teachers should be familiar with the distinction between tests designed to measure aptitude and tests designed to measure achievement. Today's accountability tests are almost always achievement tests although, in a few settings (and thanks to debatable logic), aptitude tests have actually been proposed for use as accountability tests.

Selected-Response and Constructed-Response Tests

The advantage of tests composed of selected-response items—the most common of which are multiple-choice items and binary-choice items (like True/False or Right/Wrong)—is that they can cover a substantial amount of content in a relatively brief time. Students' responses can also be scored rather rapidly. On the negative side, because students can choose their responses from an already presented array of options, it's possible for students to perform relatively well on such items even when their mastery of what's being tested may fall short of the teacher's goal.

A more direct and, therefore, usually more nuanced exemplification of students' covert skills and knowledge can be obtained through the use of *constructed-response items*, the most common of which are *short-answer items* and *essay items*. The downside of constructed-response items is that they take substantial time to score and, unless scored with considerable care, sometimes yield unreliable and inaccurate data. These days, constructed responses are almost always scored with a rubric, and it's important to remember that rubrics can vary substantially in quality.

Over the past decade or so, two variations of constructed-response items have found widespread favor among educators: performance tests and portfolio assessment. In a *performance test*, students undertake a formidable task (say, writing a 1,000-word narrative essay), and then the teacher (or somebody else) makes a judgment about students' task mastery. In *portfolio assessment*, students' constructed responses are collected over a substantial time period and evaluated chiefly on the basis of each student's overall, portfolio-documented improvement relative to the skill or skills being assessed. Both performance tests and portfolio assessments possess considerable potential. However, both approaches also require meaningful effort if they are to work properly.

Affective Assessments

Students' affect—their attitudes, interests, and values—is a remarkably important aspect of education, and setting out to measure it through affective assessment is fundamentally different from measuring students' status with respect to cognitive skills or knowledge. When dealing with cognitive curricular aims, we typically possess assessment tools that can provide evidence to support a reasonably accurate, if less than perfectly precise, inference about a particular student's status. In contrast, when trying to gauge students' attitudes, interests, and values, we just don't possess assessment tools sufficiently accurate to ascertain a *particular* student's affective status.

Thus, the mission of affective measuring instruments is to help teachers arrive at an inference about a group of students, typically a teacher's class or, at the secondary level, each of a teacher's classes. These group-focused inferences are intended to help teachers make decisions about the affect-related instructional procedures they're providing for all of their students rather than make affect-related instructional decisions for a particular student. In other words, the point is not to help a teacher decide whether Johnny is interested in science or Jill hates mathematics. As you will read in Chapter 4, the most practical method of securing information about the affective status of a student group is to employ *anonymous, self-report inventories,* in which students register agreement or disagreement with a series of statements related to affective variables, such as attitude toward school or interest in particular subjects. Clearly, when students respond anonymously to a self-report inventory, we can't tell which student completed which inventory, so the possibility of deriving assessment-based inferences about individual students simply goes out the window.

Most experts who have worked in the arena of affective assessment believe the best approach to the measurement of students' affect is some variation on the attitudinal assessment scheme developed more than 70 years ago by Rensis Likert (1932). Likert's method calls for individuals to register their degree of agreement with a variety of positively and negatively phrased statements. Figure 2.1 shows an example of a Likert-like inventory for elementary teachers who wish to get a fix on their students' attitudes toward several content areas and skills related to those content areas. If teachers discover their students are positively disposed to most subject areas (or skills related to them) but are negatively disposed toward one particular subject, such as mathematics, then the teachers can provide class activities intended to make students' attitudes toward math more positive.

Figure 2.1	A Likert-Like Affective Inventory for Elementary Students

Directions: Please indicate whether you agree, disagree, or are uncertain about each of the statements below this box. Some of the statements are worded positively, and some are worded negatively. For each statement, show how you feel about that statement by placing an X in one of the three boxes for that statement. There are no right or wrong answers, so please answer honestly based on how *you feel*. Do not write your name or make comments on this paper. Only make X marks.

	Agree	**Disagree**	**Uncertain**
I like to watch TV in the evening.	☒	☐	☐

When you have finished, a student will collect this sheet and place it and all other completed sheets in an envelope that will be taken to the office. Thanks for your help.

	Agree	Disagree	Uncertain
1. I like to watch TV in the evening.	☐	☐	☐
2. Usually, I don't like to work with math problems.	☐	☐	☐
3. I look forward to the times we study science in class.	☐	☐	☐
4. I really don't have a good time when we read things.	☐	☐	☐
5. If I have to speak in front of the class, I don't like it.	☐	☐	☐
6. Doing scientific things in class bores me.	☐	☐	☐
7. I love it when we get to read stuff in class.	☐	☐	☐
8. I truly don't like it when we have to write things in class.	☐	☐	☐
9. Doing mathematics in class is something I like.	☐	☐	☐
10. I enjoy giving oral reports in class.	☐	☐	☐

As you can see in the figure, there are 10 statements in total, with 2 statements (1 positive and 1 negative) related to each of the following topics: writing, reading, oral communication, mathematics, and science. If students are positively disposed toward science, for example, they would tend to agree with Statement 3 and disagree with Statement 6. Scoring students' responses is a matter of computing a score for each *pair* of statements, assigning (for example) two points for an "agree" response to a positively phrased statement, one point for an "uncertain" response to that item, and zero points for a "disagree" response to that positively phrased statement. For a negatively phrased statement, you would weight the scale in the opposite direction: assigning two points to a "disagree" response, one point to an "uncertain" response, and zero points to an "agree" response. Thus, for each pair of items on the inventory, a student could earn from zero to four points, with higher scores reflecting more positive dispositions toward the topic addressed. For each of the five affective dimensions addressed in Figure 2.1's illustrative inventory, you could calculate "percent of available points earned" in a fashion similar to the following:

Focus of Item-Pair	Percent of Available Points
Writing	86%
Reading	91%
Oral Communication	51%
Mathematics	43%
Science	76%

Now, if a teacher were to administer an anonymous affective inventory during the third month of the school year and find numbers like these, the results would suggest that teacher should alter his or her approach to mathematics and oral communication instruction. For some reason, what's been going on for the past three months is not connecting with students.

Teachers who wish to do so might use a five-response scheme including "strongly agree," "agree," "uncertain," disagree," and "strongly disagree." In this instance, the teacher would assign zero to four points *per item* based on whether the item's statement was phrased positively or negatively. The total for a *pair* of items, then, could range between zero and eight points. Also, it is not necessary to use the "uncertain" response option at all, although most Likert-like inventories do employ it. Remember, this sort of affective assessment is really a "rough and dirty" sort of educational assessment that, measurement precision notwithstanding, is intended to help focus a teacher's attention on a set of remarkably important educational consequences: students' attitudes, interests, and values.

There are certainly other ways—lots of them, in fact—to classify educational assessment devices. However, these three educational assessment categories—aptitude/achievement tests, selected-response/constructed-response, and affective assessment—should be sufficiently serviceable. If any of these topics tantalize you into learning more about them, check out the nifty Suggestions for Further Reading at the chapter's close.

Now, let's tie a ribbon around this one-and-only assessment-focused chapter by dealing with a final measurement issue with considerable relevance to instruction.

The Summative and Formative Functions of Educational Assessments

More than 40 years ago, Michael Scriven (1967) made a major contribution to the field of educational evaluation when he introduced a particularly useful distinction between the *formative evaluation* of educational programs and the *summative evaluation* of these same programs. Formative evaluations of an educational program, for instance, an under development peer-tutoring system, were to be carried out while the program was still malleable and, therefore, capable of being improved as a consequence of the evaluation. Summative evaluations were to be carried out for final-version educational programs, such as a series of computer-delivered geometry lessons, so that a definitive go/no-go decision could be reached regarding whether the program should continue.

Through the years, increasing numbers of educators have begun analogously applying those two labels to educational assessment. *Summative assessment*, as you might infer, describes the sort of testing that's used to determine how successful an instructional intervention has been or to tell how well a student has learned something. Accountability testing has been used in an unarguably summative role. *Formative assessment*, however, has been defined in a number of ways, not all of which are especially helpful for purposes of instructional decision making.

There is now ample empirical evidence that when classroom testing is used as part of a formative assessment process, substantial payoffs in learning take place. Given the considerable research evidence confirming the learning dividends of classroom formative assessment, coupled with the pervasive pressure to "get accountability test scores up," it is not surprising that a number of commercial vendors have been plastering a "formative" label on almost all of their for-sale products. Formative assessment is increasingly being regarded as a good thing to do. But what exactly *is* formative assessment, really?

> *Formative assessment* is a planned process in which assessment-elicited evidence of students' status is used by teachers to adjust their ongoing instructional procedures or by students to adjust their current learning tactics.[2]

This definition is one I use in a book devoted exclusively to formative assessment (Popham, 2008), and it draws heavily from a similar definition generated by a consortium of American educators eager to define formative assessment in terms consonant with the research corroborating this kind of assessment's instructional virtues (Council of Chief State School Officers, 2006).

There are a couple critical points to be made about my definition of formative assessment. First, note that it indicates formative assessment is not a kind of test but a process—and a *planned* process at that. Moreover, that planned process revolves around the collection of assessment-elicited evidence. Based on such evidence, either teachers make adjustments in how they are teaching, or students make adjustments in how they are trying to learn. Teachers will discover that if they fully embrace the use of formative assessment as they monitor the ongoing quality of their instruction, formative assessment can truly transform how they teach. We will consider this fascinating topic more fully in Chapter 5.

---

[2] I have profited from conversations with three good friends and respected colleagues, Lorrie Shepard, Rick Stiggins, and Dylan Wiliam, regarding the precise wording of an appropriate definition of formative assessment. Any shortcomings in this definition are mine, not theirs.

✔ Chapter Check-Back

- Educational assessment is an inference-making activity in which educators base interpretations about students' covert status on those students' overt test performances.

- An educational test's usefulness for particular assessment functions should be judged according to the following four factors: reliability, validity, bias, and instructional sensitivity.

- Although educational assessment devices can be categorized in a variety of ways, educators should be familiar with aptitude versus achievement tests, constructed-response and selected-response items, and how to assess students' affect.

- Educators should be familiar with the distinction between summative and formative assessment and also with the potent role formative assessment can play in improving instructional quality.

Suggestions for Further Reading

Frisbie, D. A. (2005, Fall). Presidential address: Measurement 101: Some fundamentals revisited. *Educational Measurement: Issues and Practice, 24*(5), 21–28.

In his outgoing address as president of the National Council on Educational Measurement, Frisbie lays out a set of basics in educational assessment—concepts that he feels have been distorted in recent years. The article gives teachers a list of important misconceptions to avoid.

Pellegrino, J. W., Chudowsky, N., & Glaser, R. (Eds.). (2001). *Knowing what students know: The science and design of educational assessment.* Washington, DC: National Academy Press.

This influential volume from the Board on Testing and Assessment, affiliated with the National Research Council's Division of Behavioral and Social Sciences and Education's Center for Education, presents a strategy for designing educational tests in accord with cognitive psychology's current conceptions of human learning. Because the volume has influenced many assessment special-ists' sense of how best to assess learners, it is a worthwhile read for educators who care about the defensible measurement of what students know.

Popham, W. J. (2008). *Classroom assessment: What teachers need to know* (5th ed.). Needham Heights, MA: Allyn & Bacon.

This is the fifth edition of a widely used classroom assessment textbook writ-ten by yours truly. It provides a more detailed treatment of each of the topics addressed in this chapter.

Schmoker, M. (2008/2009, December/January). Measuring what matters. *Educational Leadership, 66*(4), 70–74.

In this analysis, Schmoker argues that schools must collect data designed to serve a 21st century agenda. He describes the accomplishments of a consortium of 28 New York high schools that have evolved a data-driven decision-making approach intended to promote students' mastery of more defensible cognitive outcomes. Activities of the consortium, described in this essay, are worthy of readers' consideration.

Stiggins, R. J. (2007). *An introduction to student-involved assessment for learning* (5th ed.). Upper Saddle River, NJ: Prentice-Hall.

Although Stiggins addresses the traditional collection of measurement constructs, he does so in the context of how a classroom can operate when it is oriented around a formative assessment conception of learning.

3

Curriculum
Determination

A teacher's instructional decision making ought to revolve around a simple ends-means model. First, a teacher determines which ends to pursue: which sets of skills, knowledge, or affect the students should acquire. Thereafter, the teacher designs and implements instructional activities, monitors those activities to see if they need to be adjusted, and finally evaluates the effectiveness of the adjusted or unadjusted instructional activities. The four steps in this approach to instruction, then, are (1) curriculum determination, (2) design/delivery of instruction, (3) monitoring of instruction, and (4) evaluation of instruction. When you strip away the frills, this four-step process is what teaching is all about.

The more clearheaded teachers are when carrying out this ends-means strategy, the more successful their instruction will be. However, all the rigorous instructional thinking in the world is wasted if teachers promote the mastery of the *wrong* curricular ends. In this chapter, we're going to be looking at how to choose the curricular ends that should govern all of a teacher's subsequent means-related instructional decisions.

About now, many of you are probably thinking, "*Choose* the curricular ends? In my district, curricular ends are chosen *for* me!" In more and more educational settings, this is indeed the case. Teachers are supposed to promote an official set of authorized curricular aims handed down by the district, the state, the province, or some other governing entity. And teachers usually find that one or more annual accountability tests have been installed to determine how much success they have had getting their students to achieve the externally stipulated curricular ends. But, as I hinted in Chapter 1, the way that governmentally imposed curricular aspirations are assessed can make a huge difference in the degree to which teachers must toe the curricular line.

As you read on, you'll see my position regarding curricular choices is one that runs counter to the preferences of some governmental authorities. Teachers, you can make up your own mind regarding whether my argument for subtle curricular insubordination is sound enough to accept. Administrators and supervisors, you, too, will have to arrive at your own decision about whether you wish to tolerate or perhaps even endorse a dash of curricular insurrection. With that bit of provocation laid out, let's get to it.

A Consideration of Curriculum Constraints

It's been a long, long while since teachers had total autonomy when choosing curricular aims for their students. Oh, I imagine Socrates felt free to decide on his curricular aims for Plato, and Plato surely had oceans of independence when it came to determining curricular outcomes for Aristotle. But teachers' curricular autonomy has been drastically diminished since then, especially in recent years.

Curricular constraints, at least in some form, make good sense. Rather than have teachers aim their instructional activities at a host of diverse outcomes, why not provide those teachers with some curricular guidance? Indeed, prestigious groups of prominent educators and national associations of subject-matter specialists have long taken the view that both teachers and students benefit from some direction when it comes to curriculum. What's changed over the past few decades is that governmental agencies—at federal, state, provincial, and local levels—have gotten increasingly involved in determining what students should learn and when they should learn it.

This too, in itself, is not necessarily a bad thing. Almost all the resulting official curricular documents reflect the input of seasoned educators with special expertise in a given subject area. It is altogether reasonable to assemble committees of thoughtful, knowledgeable experts in language arts, mathematics, science, and so on, and then ask them to lay out a set of worthwhile curricular outcomes for students. However, those pronouncements can sometimes induce teachers to adopt a stance of curricular acquiescence. This is problematic, because although some of today's collections of curricular aims are unarguably excellent, many fall several notches below that standard. There are two key reasons for this: *a lack of curricular clarity* and *too many curricular aims.*

A lack of curricular clarity. The statements of curricular aims expressed in these collections are often insufficiently explicit for purposes of instructional planning. If a teacher can't make out what a curricular aim means, how will that teacher go about teaching it? For an illustration of this point, take a look at two official curricular standards snared from a U.S. state department of education Web site:

> *Civics:* The student understands and applies knowledge of government, law, politics, and the nation's fundamental documents to make decisions about local, national, and international issues and to demonstrate thoughtful, participatory citizenship.

> *Geography:* The student uses a spatial perspective to make reasoned decisions by applying the concepts of location, region, and movement and demonstrating knowledge of how geographic features and human cultures impact environments.

Okay, after reading these descriptions and taking some time to digest them (possibly with the help of some bicarbonate of soda), do you understand these two curricular aims well enough to devise an instructional sequence that would get students to achieve the ends these aims articulate? Well, I sure as heck don't, and I even taught civics and geometry once upon a time. If you care to replicate my little excursion into Internet standards-snaring, just go to the Web site of almost any U.S. state or Canadian province and there you'll find a spate of curricular aims not all that different from the two I've listed here. What I contend is that such aims are insufficiently clear to permit on-target instructional planning.

Too many curricular aims. The second drawback of these well-intentioned collections is that they tend to be incredibly lengthy. Here's another example of a curricular aim taken from the same state's Web site. It is one of six mathematics content standards for the state's 7th graders:

> Students extend their understanding of surface area and volume to include finding surface area and volume of cylinders and volume of cones and pyramids. They apply formulas and solve a range of problems involving three-dimensional objects, including problems people encounter in everyday life, in certain types of work and in other school subjects. With a strong understanding of how to work with both two-dimensional and three-dimensional figures, students build an important foundation for the geometry they will study in high school.

Now, as I said, this state's 7th graders have only six total mathematics standards, and a half-dozen standards—even standards that are as wordy as the one above—doesn't sound all that bad. It doesn't sound all that bad *until* we realize that each of the six standards has its own list of "performance expectations": all the stuff a student is supposed to be able to do in order to show attainment of that standard. When one looks closely at those performance expectations, it turns out that the six standards subsume fully 35 separate performance expectations. And that's 35 curricular expectations for students in just one subject: math.

While I was doing my curricular cruising on the Internet, I looked up the curricular expectations for a 4th grade teacher in a second unnamed U.S. state and discovered that if you are teaching 4th grade kids in this mystery state, you are officially responsible for promoting students' achievement of 299 potentially assessable curricular aims. Talk about curricular absurdity. It's simply not possible for teachers to teach all of these curricular aims during a single school year—or, rather, it's not possible to teach them with the kind of rigor likely to foster deep and lasting learning.

So, although I believe teachers should definitely look at the curricular recommendations promulgated by prestigious education organizations and government agencies, it would be a mistake for teachers to automatically regard any of these sets as the final word on what should be taught and learned in their classrooms. Yes, teachers should read these curricular recommendations and requirements. Yes, teachers should consider them, investigate them, and discuss them with colleagues. But then teachers should make up their own minds if these curricular aims are to be the ones they want their students to master.

Of course, it's not *quite* that simple. There's another factor teachers need to consider when encountering curricular proclamations, and that's the degree of "classroom bite" associated with these documents. Curricular recommendations from nongovernmental groups, such as subject-area associations, are just that: *recommendations*. For teachers, there's no obligation to do anything *but* consider them—exactly as teachers might consider the expert advice of veteran colleagues. *Governmental* curricular constraints, however, can be quite another matter. Yes, sometimes they are meant to function only in a heuristic role—simply to encourage teachers to consider a wider range of curricular outcomes than teachers might have done otherwise. But the vast majority of today's governmentally issued collections of curricular outcomes *are supposed to be followed*, without deviation.

Very often there is governmental scrutiny of the match between the mandated curricular goals and what really goes on in classrooms. School-site administrators are urged by higher-level administrators to guarantee that teachers are promoting these officially endorsed curricular aims. Teachers are continually reminded to be sure their instructional activities are "in alignment" with official curricular goals. In some places, government inspectors actually visit classrooms to determine if this alignment is in place. In *most* places where curricular outcomes are mandated, a test focused on the assessment of these outcomes is administered to students as a way to hold teachers accountable both for teaching the outcomes and for teaching them well.

The broader and more general the official curricular aim, the more likely it is that teachers' instructional activities will meet the official alignment standard. For example, with a large-grain mathematics curricular aim such as "Numeration," it's probable that many of a teacher's numerically oriented activities will be seen as in alignment. However, if the official curriculum document breaks the Numeration goal into more specific, smaller-grain curricular aims (for example, "Thousands," "Fractions," or "Decimals"), then a governmentally appointed observer might more readily discover a lack of alignment between what goes on in class and what the government says *should* go on in class.

Thus, the first choice teachers face when they think about the practical selection of curricular goals for their students hinges heavily on whether they, *personally*, are under pressure to align day-to-day classroom activities with the outcomes set forth in a governmental collection of curricular aims. If they aren't, they can take one path toward curriculum determination; if they are, they need to take another.

What I'll be describing in the remainder of this chapter is how educators can choose curricular aims in two very different settings. The first of these, less common than most of us would prefer, finds educators free to make curricular decisions on the basis of what is educationally best for their students. In the other setting, the presence of governmentally determined curricular constraints (and accompanying accountability tests) limits a teacher's options. Frankly, in today's era of educational accountability, I think most educators are functioning in the second situation—a situation loaded with potent curricular constraints. Even so, I need you to understand how it is that a teacher who does not have total freedom regarding what to teach can still be attentive to the significant choice-points in how to carry out a defensible search for what curricular targets we should be aiming at for kids. Teachers with moxie can make the best of the curricular hand they've been dealt by incorporating at least parts of a defensible curriculum determination process into their practice.

Curriculum Determination in an Unconstrained Environment

Let's assume, for the sake of illustration, you're a teacher in a situation where there are few constraints on the curricular aims you can choose for your students. Perhaps you teach in a private school, at the college level, or in a school where governmental curricular documents are officially in place but have little bite. Given free or relatively free rein to arrive at a set of curricular aims, how should you go about making your selection?

I recommend a four-step process, shown in Figure 3.1.

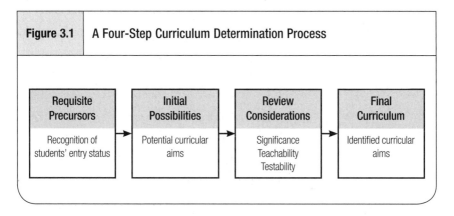

| Figure 3.1 | A Four-Step Curriculum Determination Process |

Requisite Precursors	Initial Possibilities	Review Considerations	Final Curriculum
Recognition of students' entry status	Potential curricular aims	Significance Teachability Testability	Identified curricular aims

Step 1: Recognizing students' entry status. Curricular planning is not an abstract enterprise; it's choosing curricular aims for a particular collection of kids: the kids being taught. Accordingly, it would be foolish to identify a set of curricular aims without considering whether those aims will be suitable for the specific group of students a teacher finds in class.

There are two obvious but nonetheless important questions a teacher must ask here: (1) *Do my students already possess the skills, knowledge, or affect comprising this curricular aim?* and (2) *Is this curricular aim too advanced for my students—that is, do they have the foundational skills or bodies of knowledge necessary to pursue it?*

Sometimes answers to these questions will be readily at hand. Within a month or two (and almost certainly by midyear), most teachers have become conversant with their students' general strengths and weaknesses. This familiarity with students' knowledge, skills, and affect will provide the insight needed to narrow the pool of potentially suitable curricular aims for the second semester. But at the beginning of the school year, with a classroom full of students whose abilities are unknown, assessment is the best bet for clarifying just what a group of brand new students is bringing to class.

The teacher should begin by focusing on something known: the sorts of curriculum aims that are under consideration. A 5th grade teacher might not yet know which specific language arts aims will be most appropriate for her incoming group of students, but she can look to the aims she and her 5th graders pursued last year as a starting point. With last year's aims in front of her, she can devise a pre-test to measure the incoming students' status relative to those aims as well as the critical subskills and bodies of enabling knowledge.

Because the purpose of this assessment is to gauge the general entry status of the students as a group, there is no reason to administer the assessment to every student. A procedure known as *item-sampling* will generate the needed insight without eating too deeply into instructional time. Instead of requiring an entire class of 24 students to spend an entire class period completing a 40-item pre-assessment, a teacher could split the 40-item test into 4 quick-to-complete 10-item subtests, and then randomly administer each subtest to a quarter of the students. Securing a sufficiently accurate estimate of the entry status of the entire class would then be a simple matter of amalgamating the results.

Step 2: Identifying potential curricular aims. After a teacher has arrived at a reasonable idea about students' entry-level skills, knowledge, and affect, it's time to come up with a preliminary set of worthy curricular aims. I have two pieces of advice to share here.

Consider the curricular counsel of others but don't meekly succumb to it. Sets of expert curricular recommendations from organizations such as the National Council of Teachers of English or the National Council of

Teachers of Mathematics are worthy of review, as even the most experienced teacher can find worthwhile ideas in these groups' curricular counsel. But, as professionals exercising professional judgment, teachers who have the freedom to select the curricular aims that will best serve their students should exercise that freedom and make the final decision themselves. This is not just a philosophical argument but a practical one. As noted, the published recommendations of curricular groups tend to be "wish lists" of all the wonderful things they would like students to know and be able to do. Actual pursuit of all these curricular aims over the course of a school year is manifestly unfeasible in any real-world classroom.

Select only a modest, intellectually manageable number of curricular targets and decide on a "grain-size" that is teachable. A teacher who decides to concentrate instructional attention on the accomplishment of, say, a half-dozen curricular aims will typically be able to do so and do so effectively. In contrast, a teacher who opts to concentrate instructional attention on the accomplishment of, say, 40 or 50 curricular targets has probably taken on an impossible task. Effective promotion of any curricular aim requires time: time to craft a well-thought-out instructional plan and time to deliver that plan. Too many curricular aims crowd out a teacher's instructional clarity, hampering that teacher's ability to teach the most important things really well.

If you are a teacher concerned that you won't be able to give all the curricular ends you have in mind the proper degree of attention, then you should either (1) reduce that number of curricular aims or (2) reformulate those aims at a larger *grain-size*, which is another way of saying *expand their scope.* It is far better for students to master a modest number of truly potent, large-grain curricular aims than it is for them to superficially touch on a galaxy of smaller-grain curricular aims. With a bit of additional thought, a collection of smaller-scope curricular aims can be coalesced into a single, larger-scope curricular aim.

When I was a first-year teacher, I taught an 11th grade English class and followed the curricular course set in our blessed textbook. It told me that there would be a four-week unit on "Oral Communication," in which I was supposed to help my students become better at making oral presentations. Because I had not taught 11th grade English previously (well, I had not taught *anything* previously), I plotted out my instructional plan by identifying all the things I wanted students to work on before I asked them to make an end-of-unit extemporaneous speech to their classmates. This list included (1) good eye contact, (2) good posture, (3) appropriate gestures, (4) inclusion of sufficient content, (5) suitable organization of presentation, (6) an attention-getting introduction, and (7) a powerful conclusion. I know there actually were another five of these separate little evaluative factors, because I recall that I employed an even dozen factors when I graded students' practice and final speeches. The trouble is that I can't remember the other five factors. I suspect that many students couldn't recall them, either.

What I *should* have done is take my dozen attributes and boil them down to three or four things that my students could really remember well enough to incorporate into their speech preparation. I broke the unit into too many unpalatable beans when what I should have been doing is serving a tasty bean dip. The truth is, teachers, and students, can concentrate their attention sensibly on only a half-dozen or so curricular targets. In the curricular grain-size game, less is most definitely more.

Of course, it's important not to expand the grain-size of a curricular aim to the point that the aim's clarity is sacrificed. An example of a too-broad curricular aim is "Students will learn about pivotal political issues." Another example of a broad-scope curricular aim gone bonkers is "Students will become good communicators." A simple way to find out if the grain-size of any curricular aim has become too large is simply to run that aim by several colleagues, preferably at different times. Ask them to tell you what the curricular aim really means. If the responses you get are quite similar, the grain-size of the curricular aim is probably fine. If your colleagues' responses diverge significantly, then you've expanded your grain-size too much.

In addition to asking colleagues, teachers can toss a few questions at themselves in an attempt to spot overweight curricular aims:

- What does the curricular aim really mean?
- How can I measure students' mastery of it?
- Can I explain the aim to students?
- How long will it take me to truly get students to master this aim?
- Is this curricular aim really understandable or just a romp in rhetoric?

When it comes to the number of curricular aims a teacher should be pursuing, much depends on grade level. Elementary teachers, who are almost always responsible for dealing with several subjects, face a tougher task than their secondary-level colleagues, who likely teach only one. Mrs. Pell, a high school geometry teacher, might identify 10 key curricular aims that all of her geometry classes will pursue. She feels certain that she can concentrate instructionally on those 10 aims and that if her students achieve all of the 10 aims, they will have learned what they truly need to know about high school geometry. In contrast, Mr. Peavy, a 2nd grade teacher, must teach reading, writing, mathematics, social studies, science, and the arts. If he were to identify 10 curricular aims for each of these 6 subjects, he'd end up with 60 aims overall—way too many to address with sufficient instructional intensity to promote deep mastery. Thus, teachers who are responsible for multiple-subject instruction need to be especially careful to adopt a less-is-more approach to curriculum determination. They must be unrelentingly honest with themselves: *For every curricular aim I'm considering, can I devise effective instruction, provide that instruction, and then assess students' meaningful mastery?* A teacher who can answer "yes" to this multipart question has most likely arrived at a suitable number of potential curricular aims.

Step 3: Reviewing and evaluating the collection of potential curricular aims. With a pool of potentials now identified, there are three evaluative criteria a teacher should use to judge the final suitability of each curricular aim under consideration. They are the aim's *significance*, its *teachability*, and its *testability*.

Significance. The significance of a curricular aim refers to its importance for the students being taught. Thus, for younger students, teachers usually find the significance of a curricular aim arises from the kind of contribution that mastery of this aim will make to children's subsequent schooling. Consider how significant a 4th grader's mastery of positive and negative numbers is to this student's subsequent mastery of more advanced mathematics content. For older students, the importance of a curricular aim is often influenced more heavily by whether its mastery will contribute to a student's well-being in the workplace or as a member of society.

Every teacher should scrutinize every potential curricular aim and make a personal decision about that aim's importance. It's a matter of asking questions like these:

- Does this curricular aim mesh with my own instructional values? Does it reflect what I think is important?

- Based on my experience and training, is this the kind of skill students must have to support their subsequent schooling or life in the workplace?

- What's the need for this curricular aim among this particular cohort of students? How does it mesh with their existing levels of proficiency?

- Is the affective goal reflected in this curricular aim likely to have a beneficial effect on this particular group of students?

Because smaller numbers of high-import curricular aims are preferable to a truck-load of low-import curricular aims, teachers might wish to prioritize the potential curricular aims they've identified. It's a simple matter of *ranking* all of the potential aims according to how important the teacher feels each aim to be. What's more, this ranking exercise often helps teachers discover that, while most of their potential curricular aims are *truly* significant, a few could be excised with minimal effect.

Another helpful hint for determining a curricular aim's significance is this simple credo: "If it's nice to know, it's got to go!" In other words, if an under-consideration curricular aim is only "nice to know" rather than *essential* for students to achieve, then such an aim should be sent sauntering. The world is full of knowledge, skills, understandings, and attitudes that we would love our students to acquire, if only there were time enough. But there isn't. Prioritizing a set of potential curricular aims on the basis of their genuine significance to the students involved is a way for teachers to decide if these aims truly are worth pursuing instructionally.

Teachability. At the same time teachers are considering their potential curricular aims from a significance perspective, they can also look at each of those aims in terms of *teachability.* More precisely, this evaluative criterion refers to the likelihood that teachers will be able to successfully promote a particular curricular aim in the instructional time available to promote their students' mastery of that aim. To apply this second evaluative criterion, then, teachers need to have at least a ballpark idea of how many days, weeks, or months of instructional time they can realistically devote to getting their students to master a given curricular aim. Clearly, if a teacher doesn't have enough time to teach students to acquire a certain high-level cognitive skill, then it is silly to identify students' acquisition of this cognitive skill as a curricular aim. First-rate instruction is not a game of instructional fantasy; it requires frank, rigorous estimation of what can be done to benefit students in the instructional time available.

Teachers attempting to discern if the curricular aim under consideration is one that can realistically be taught might ask themselves questions such as the following:

• How much time will it take me to teach students to master the component parts of this aim?

• What is the minimum length of instructional time this aim will require, and what is the maximum length of time it will require?

• Given the other curricular aims I must pursue, do I really have time to accomplish this curricular aim?

Here's a simple example of how determining the teachability of a curricular aim might work. Suppose you are a middle school English teacher, and it's important to you that your students become proficient writers, capable of generating effective written compositions. However, you also want your students to become adept at other forms of communication, including listening and giving oral presentations. In your initial set of potential curricular aims for those students, you might include the following written-composition objective: "Students will become proficient in their ability to compose narrative, descriptive, expository, and persuasive essays." Yet, as you give more thought to the various communication skills you want your students to acquire, you conclude that focusing on all four composition genres would be a serious mistake. You might be able to *introduce* your students to all four kinds of essay writing, but your students would not have time to become *skilled* in all four genres. Given such an analysis, and seeing how your original curricular aim about composition would most certainly founder on the evaluative criterion of teachability, you could sensibly choose to pursue only *one* of the four genres of writing: expository essay writing, perhaps. You might have chosen expository essay writing because you recognized how important being able to explain events and processes will be to your middle schoolers' future efforts in social studies, science, and English classes. Focusing on that one kind of writing vastly increases the odds that you will be able to teach your students to be skillful writers. More important, you'll have time to tackle your other significant curricular aims: the additional forms of communication you want your students to master.

It should be apparent that applying the teachability evaluative criterion to potential curricular aims involves taking a careful look at the entire set of those potential aims. If one or two of these aims are going to require gobs of teaching time, there will be fewer teaching-time gobs available for the other aims. After estimating the teaching time you'll need for each potential curricular aim, and then estimating the overall teaching time needed to deal with the complete set of your potential curricular aims, you'll frequently find there's a need for some tough-love prioritizing and, thereafter, pruning.

Testability. The crux of this final evaluative criterion is the question of whether students' attainment of a curricular aim can be accurately assessed through practical, real-world testing, such as the routine sorts of classroom assessments described in Chapter 2.

There are two reasons it's important for a curricular aim to be testable. First, when using an ends-means conception of instruction, it is imperative to know whether the chosen instructional means truly resulted in students' achievement of the curricular ends being pursued. And the only way to get an accurate fix on a curricular aim's achievement is to determine whether students have actually attained it. Thus, every target a teacher identifies as a curricular contender must definitely be assessable.

The second reason the testability of a potential curricular aim can be helpful to a teacher stems from the additional *clarity of intent* achieved through embodying a curricular aim in the form of students' performances on one or more assessments. (Remember, because tests are used to make inferences about students' covert status, multiple measures of this status invariably permit better test-based inferences than reliance on a single measure.) Tests, as *exemplifications* of a curricular aim, provide teachers with illustrative clarity about what they're seeking from their students. Such clarity will really pay off when the teacher gets around to planning actual instructional activities. We'll look more closely at this in Chapter 4.

You need to realize that not all worthwhile curricular aims will necessarily lend themselves to assessment. For instance, I've seen some teachers trying to get their students to be adept at "group problem solving." This is a laudable curricular aim, simply smacking of 21st century skills. Nonetheless, as a practical matter, assessing students' mastery of this high-level skill is truly difficult for most teachers to pull off by themselves.

To get a fix on a curricular aim's testability, teachers might pose the following kinds of questions to themselves:

- What sort of assessment, or assessments, will I be able to use to tell whether my students have achieved this curricular aim?
- Do I have sufficient time at my disposal to create the necessary assessments to determine if my students have achieved this curricular aim?
- Do I realistically have enough time to score students' responses to the assessment approach I am considering, without sacrificing my own sanity or longevity?

- Will I need to involve others in the scoring of these assessment instruments and, if so, can I secure such involvement?

By answering these and similar queries, teachers can arrive at a judgment about whether a potential curricular aim is genuinely assessable. Remember, in most instances, unassessed curricular aims turn out to be little more than high-sounding talk. Teachers must be certain that students' attainment of potential curricular aims can be accurately and efficiently measured.

Step 4: Adopting the curriculum. With the evaluation process complete, the teacher is left with a well-reasoned, defensible curriculum: a set of appropriate, significant, teachable, and testable curricular aims addressing skills, knowledge, and affect. These are the final curricular ends that, beaconlike, should guide all of a teacher's subsequent instructional planning.

Practical Curriculum Determination for Curricularly Constrained Times

Let's return now to the world most educators live and work in—the one in which teachers are told not only that they must promote students' mastery of a set of officially authorized curricular aims but also that students' attainment of those aims, assessed each year via instructionally insensitive accountability tests, will be the measure of teachers' own instructional effectiveness, and of their school's.

We know that such accountability-oriented settings can be both high pressure and educationally worrisome, in that desperate teachers sometimes adopt instructional practices that are unarguably damaging to students. Some of these test-pressured teachers might engage in *curricular reductionism,* wherein they devote little or no instructional time to any curricular aim not included on annual accountability tests and, thus, shortchange students. Other test-pressured teachers force their students to participate in *excessive test-preparation* activities, wherein hours and hours of classroom time are devoted to testlike practice activities. Such test-prep drudgery drains the joy from students' learning. And there are even some educators who engage in *modeled dishonesty,* taking serious ethical shortcuts when readying their students for accountability tests or when administering those tests. Most educators are definitely not doing these deplorable things. However, if only *one* educator is taking part in curricular reductionism, excessive test-preparation, or modeled dishonesty, that's one educator too many.

The majority of teachers working under curricular constraints and accountability pressure are simply trying to do the best job they can. They want to provide their students with an excellent education, but they also recognize the "don't rock the boat" pragmatism of complying with what the authorities have told them to do. And so they'll try to address the too-many curricular aims, and, having made calculated guesses about what's likely to be covered on a given year's accountability test, they'll hope their students' test scores will somehow improve. In many professions, this sort of compliance with official dictates makes sense.

But "doing what one is supposed to do" doesn't cut it in education. We dare not succumb to a compliance-at-any-cost curricular stance if that posture harms children. And it will.

It is for this reason I recommend teachers *not* try to get their students to master all the curricular aims they are supposed to have them master. Similarly, I recommend teachers *not* try to orient their instructional activities toward what they guess will be coming up on an approaching accountability test. Both of those endeavors will be a waste of the teacher's time and, more importantly, a waste of the students' time.

Let's focus on this problem from a student's point of view. We can use a pair of binary-choice items to guide our decision making:

1. Will a student benefit more from a teacher's (a) superficially covering a hoard of curricular aims or (b) having students achieve in-depth mastery of a modest number of significant curricular aims?

2. Will a student benefit more from a teacher's focusing on (a) curricular aims that seem most likely to be tested or (b) significant curricular aims irrespective of whether these aims are assessed on an upcoming accountability test?

Is an answer key really necessary here? I thought not.

Teachers must *always* concern themselves with what's best for their students. This means playing the curricular compliance game with a certain degree of finesse. To do so, teachers need to carefully analyze the array of too-numerous official curricular aims they've been directed to promote and come up with a set of the *most important curricular aims* that can be successfully taught during the instructional time available.

As you can see, the essence of this process involves the prioritizing of potential curricular aims. For teachers trying to come up with the most important of any set of contending curricular options, there is merit in thinking back to Figure 3.1, which includes the recommendation to review potential curricular aims according to their significance, their teachability, and their testability. But remember, teachers in this instance will only have a limited number of curricular coins to spend. What this means is that teachers need to consider only those outcomes for their students that they can do a slam-bang, in-depth instructional job on. And those curricular aims must be, arguably, far and away the most important for children to acquire.

Remember, when discussing this strategy with *anyone*, especially parents and members of school boards, never—never—use the expression "narrowing the curriculum." Rather, what's going on is "prioritizing" curricular choices to ensure that students will master the most significant of those targets and master them at a depth that will be truly useful in later life. Educators who adopt this curricular stance in a patently clear effort to benefit their students need to be forthright about what they are up to, but forthrightness slathered with some serious suaveness will always work well.

As for the curricular goals that don't make this high-priority list—the ones teachers are supposed to cover, if not simply to preserve their jobs? Well, I suggest that teachers do just that: cover them. There's a huge difference between "covering" a curricular aim and tackling that same curricular aim with sufficient intensity to ensure students' deep, long-term mastery. Just to stay conscionably compliant with official mandates, teachers will need to give some attention to the curricular aims they're not focusing on. *However*, precious classroom minutes are better spent teaching students what they most need to learn.

Right now, you may be thinking there is peril in a teacher's not trying to figure out what accountability tests are assessing and then emphasizing such content in class. Actually, there's no peril—none at all. Remember, instructionally insensitive accountability tests are essentially *insensitive* to instruction, meaning what a teacher emphasizes in class is probably not going to make a substantial difference in students' scores on an instructionally insensitive accountability test. Indeed, if a teacher's students truly master a modest collection of *significant* skills and knowledge, odds are that those students will perform better on an accountability test than if the teacher had frantically tried to cover an absurd array of too many curricular aims.

As for the test-prep issue, it makes abundant sense for teachers to give their students a modest dose of generalized test-preparation advice. I think it's wise, for example, to help students learn how to use test-taking time judiciously and how to make sensible guesses for certain sorts of selected-response items. Teachers should also provide opportunities for students to become familiar with all of the types of test items they'll be encountering in the upcoming test. But I firmly believe that one or two class periods is adequate for such generalized get-ready preparation for accountability tests.

If teachers adopt the curricular stance I recommend here, their students will bring a set of well-mastered, significant capabilities to any accountability test they're asked to tackle. This deep mastery may help them score well on the test, but even if it doesn't, they will still be better educated. And that, after all, is the real goal.

Curriculum Determination in Constrained Environments with Instructionally Sensitive Accountability Tests

Teachers who are fortunate enough to be teaching in a setting where the accountability tests are instructionally sensitive face a markedly simplified process of curriculum determination. All those teachers need to do is focus their instructional activities on students' attainment of the curricular aims being assessed by the instructionally sensitive accountability test. Yes, it's basically that simple.

Because an instructionally sensitive test *will* detect effective instruction when effective instruction is present, if a teacher's instruction is effective, the consequences of that effective instruction will show up in the form of improved students' scores on the instructionally sensitive accountability test. Moreover, because in most instances an instructionally sensitive accountability test will have been deliberately created to assess only the very most significant curricular outcomes, the clarity with which these curricular targets will have been described typically makes it possible for teachers to devise instruction that is not only *effective* (whereby students attain the sought-for curricular aim) but also *efficient* (whereby students' mastery of the assessed curricular aims can be accomplished in a time-saving manner). Effective and efficient instruction allows teachers the time they need to promote students' attainment of curricular aims that are lower priority but still worthwhile.

In the next chapter, we'll be looking at the design of instruction (the means) for whatever curricular aims a teacher has chosen. But, as a final reminder, if the curricular ends chosen are unsound, all the dazzling instruction in the world won't overcome that profoundly important deficit.

 Chapter Check-Back

- Teachers who are relatively free to adopt the curricular aims of their own choosing should follow a four-step model involving recognition of students' entry status; selection of potential curricular aims; review of those potential aims for significance, teachability, and testability; and final determination.
- Teachers who are constrained by official curricular documents should direct their instruction toward a manageable number of the highest-priority curricular aims contained therein.
- Teachers in curricularly constrained environments where the accountability tests are instructionally sensitive should focus their instruction directly on students' attainment of the officially endorsed, well-defined curricular aims.

Suggestions for Further Reading

Jacobs, H. H. (Ed.). (2004). *Getting results with curriculum mapping.* Alexandria, VA: ASCD.

Jacobs and her coauthors provide a variety of ways to use the curriculum mapping process in schools and districts. Because the quality of the goals being mapped is of great concern in this process, this book helps educators deal with the defensibility of curricular aims.

Marzano, R. J., & Haystead, M. W. (2008). *Making standards useful in the classroom.* Alexandria, VA: ASCD.

Marzano and Haystead provide a practical procedure to transform standards documents into a format that classroom teachers can employ to guide their instructional decisions and, not unimportantly, to generate assessments to be used as part of the formative assessment process.

Wiggins, G., & McTighe, J. (2005). *Understanding by design* (2nd ed.). Alexandria, VA: ASCD.

Wiggins and McTighe offer a series of useful insights regarding the isolation of significant curricular aims. Their treatment of the difference between understanding and knowledge is especially illuminating. In the Understanding by Design model, "big ideas" are "inherently transferable [and] help connect discrete topics and skills" (p. 65). These important and enduring ideas serve as the kinds of curricular targets all teachers should consider.

4

Instructional Design

Operation Overlord was the code name for the Allied Forces' invasion of Normandy in June 1944. If you were to take a gander at a typical textbook description of how teachers should design instruction, you might be inclined to dub such a reading experience *Operation Overload*. When it comes to how teachers should plan their teaching, there are countless alternative approaches and endless variations—many of them championed as "research based" or "research proven."

Research reviews focused on instructional design and methodology can indeed point out tactics that appear to have a positive impact on student achievement. Robert J. Marzano, one of our field's foremost synthesizers of instructionally relevant empirical research, shares some of his findings on instructional strategies likely to maximize student learning in the widely read book *Classroom Instruction That Works* (Marzano, Pickering, & Pollock, 2001). Among the nine strategies identified are identification of similarities and differences, setting objectives and providing feedback, nonlinguistic representation, and using cooperative learning.

But, as noted in Chapter 1, research in education points us toward likelihoods, not certainties. It's certainly wise to consider and try out instructional strategies that research suggests will be effective, but there is *no* instructional strategy or tactic so potent that it is guaranteed to win out against the day-to-day diversity present in each classroom. Agreement on this issue comes from no less an authority than Marzano himself. In his excellent book *The Art and Science of Teaching* (2007), he writes

> Research will never be able to identify instructional strategies that work with every student in every class. The best research can do is tell us which strategies have a good chance (i.e., high probability) of working well with students. Individual classroom teachers must determine which strategies to employ with the right students at the right time. (p. 5)

This is why, although armed with the best and most recent research findings regarding instructional procedures, teachers will still be obliged to engage in a pile of professional artistry when formulating and delivering their instructional plans. And because one can teach the principles of art but not actual artistry, I opt for an approach to instructional planning that is simpler than most textbook presentations. As shown in Figure 4.1, it's built on just four recommendations, which take into account the reality of today's accountability-oriented educational world. I am confident that a teacher who follows these four recommendations will come up with *better instructional design decisions* and, therefore, will be a more successful teacher.

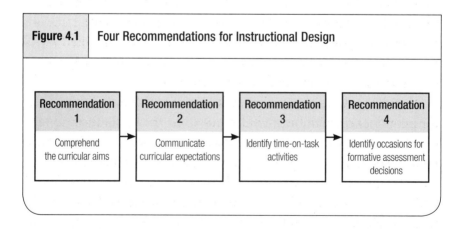

Figure 4.1   Four Recommendations for Instructional Design

Recommendation 1	Recommendation 2	Recommendation 3	Recommendation 4
Comprehend the curricular aims	Communicate curricular expectations	Identify time-on-task activities	Identify occasions for formative assessment decisions

Comprehend the Curricular Aims

The need for clear thinking by a teacher becomes particularly press-
ing when it is time to design instruction. My initial recommendation
for sound instructional design is for teachers to achieve clarity on the
outcomes they want their students to achieve. The way to do that is
to acquire a full understanding of each major curricular aim by (1)
constructing all end-of-instruction assessments before making other
instructional decisions and (2) creating a learning progression for that
curricular aim.

If teachers genuinely comprehend the essence of the curricular aim
they want their students to achieve, then it's likely those teachers' instructional designs will be more on-target than those of teachers who have
only a murky idea of where their students are headed. And that's why
this first instructional design recommendation embodies two pivotal
clarification activities.

Constructing End-of-Instruction Tests
Before Designing Instruction

Historically, teachers have built their classroom tests at the point where
instruction was winding down or actually over. And why not? When
thinking about the temporal relationships among curriculum, instruction, and assessment, most teachers first look at what to teach (curriculum), then at how to teach it (instruction), and, finally, at how to see if
students have learned what they've been taught (assessment). Figure 4.2
contrasts this typical approach, known as instruction-influenced assessment, with what I believe is a better way to handle the timing of these
critical tasks: assessment-influenced instruction.

Notice that both approaches start with curriculum: Teachers' planning commences with the intended outcomes they want their students
to achieve. But with assessment-influenced instruction, teachers create
their assessment before planning any instruction and, in so doing, they
exemplify the curricular aim or aims being sought. Teachers grapple with
and ultimately decide what mastery of those aims looks like—what its
mastery calls for a student to be able to do. It's by knowing what an aim

looks like when students display measured mastery of this aim that a teacher can decide the best means to achieve it.

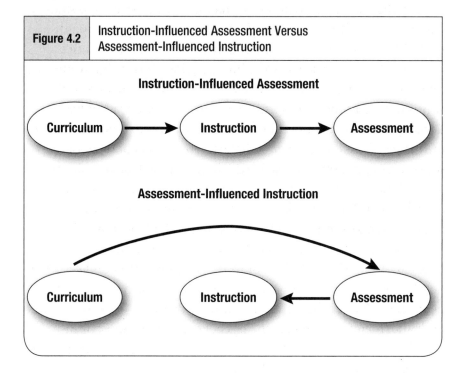

Figure 4.2 Instruction-Influenced Assessment Versus Assessment-Influenced Instruction

Instruction-Influenced Assessment

Curriculum → Instruction → Assessment

Assessment-Influenced Instruction

Curriculum   Instruction ← Assessment

Here is a simple illustration of how a teacher might think through the creation of a suitable assessment approach before planning instruction. Suppose you were setting out to teach a group of elementary students to use reference materials more effectively. Your curricular aim might be something like this: "Students will become able to efficiently obtain needed information from reference materials." This is an important skill to have—one students will be called on to use throughout their lives. Well, you might begin by thinking of the various reference materials you might provide for students to use during an assessment situation. Books? Books with indexes? Magazine and newspaper articles? Online resources? Other sources of facts and information? Once you decide which of these resources will be fair game for your test, you'd know you would need to give instructional attention to each of these materials prior to test-taking time. Getting clearheaded about an upcoming assessment is enormously helpful to teachers in determining what to emphasize instructionally.

A teacher also needs to decide the nature of the types of tasks students will be required to perform on the test. For instance, you would need to decide if your test would pre-identify a particular reference source for students to use (such as an online encyclopedia), or if it would call on students to decide which reference source among many available to consult. Beyond those important sorts of options a teacher has when devising a test to measure students' curricular aim mastery, there's also the matter of deciding format: Will the test be a paper-and-pencil one or some sort of performance test, in which students will be completing the test in the school library and using the entire array of reference materials available there? If the test is to be a paper-and-pencil one, will selected-response items or constructed-response items yield the most valid inference about students' achievement of the curricular aim?

Each of the critical choice-points that a teacher contemplates when developing an end-of-instruction assessment will help the teacher get a better cognitive handle on what is truly involved in the curricular aim itself and, therefore, will help the teacher decide what must be incorporated in any instructional plan focused on promoting students' achievement of the curricular aim under consideration.

On the most practical level, designing tests before instruction will save a teacher's time. Test construction is something that must be done anyway, but when it's done first, it helps the teacher to decide what really must go into instruction and, thus, avoid tangential topics that gobble classroom time without making a significant contribution to curricular aim mastery.

Creating a Learning Progression

Once equipped with the end-of-unit tests that will be used to assess student mastery of the curricular aim in question, a teacher should continue the pursuit of a fuller understanding of that curricular aim by creating a learning progression. For significant curricular aims, learning progression creation is a must.

A *learning progression* is a map that identifies and sequences what the teacher believes to be the "building blocks" of mastery: the particular skills and understandings a student must acquire in order to master the identified curricular aim. The construction of a learning progression is a process of discovery, something to be undertaken with scrap paper and a sharp pencil or a blank word-processing document. It can be time-consuming. However, the construction of a learning progression is a very reliable way for teachers to figure out how best to approach curricular aims instructionally, both before and during lessons. It's important enough for me to repeat: Teachers should construct at least a rudimentary learning progression for their most significant curricular aims. Doing so is a four-step process:

1. Acquire a thorough understanding of the curricular aim being sought. (We can think of it as the "target curricular aim.")

2. Identify all genuinely requisite precursory subskills and bodies of enabling knowledge. (These are the "building blocks" of the learning progression.)

3. Make certain assessment procedures can be used to measure students' status with respect to each building block.

4. Arrange all building blocks in an instructionally sound sequence.

Step 1: Understanding the target curricular aim. To me, there is no more important requisite in all of teaching than a teacher's *clarity of instructional intent*. Teachers who possess only murky understandings of the target curricular aims they are pursuing will almost certainly devise murky instructional sequences for their students. Teachers who are clearheaded about where their students are headed will almost certainly come up with more sensible instructional plans.

And this is where it pays off to have teachers develop—prior to instructional planning—the assessments they intend to use when gauging whether their students have successfully achieved a sought-for instructional outcome. For figuring out what a target curricular aim really means, there is nothing quite so helpful as constructing the assessment procedures that will determine the target curricular aim's attainment.

Step 2: Identifying the building blocks. Many educators with experience generating learning progressions report that the best way to identify a progression's building blocks is to employ a *task analysis*. Task analyses are a sort of "backward-based" thinking, reminiscent of the approach to lesson planning advocated in the book *Understanding by Design* (Wiggins & McTighe, 2005). In a task analysis, a teacher starts with the target curricular aim being sought, then identifies what students need to know and be able to do in order to master that curricular aim. The key question to answer is, *What does a student truly need to be able to do in order to do this?* What's needed may be a subskill, or it may be a chunk of key knowledge. Because target curricular aims are often significant cognitive skills, most subskills are lesser cognitive skills that students must possess before they can master the more significant target curricular aim. Bodies of enabling knowledge are typically memorized information, such as facts, principles, and rules. The task-analysis step of the process is about trying to "get into students' heads" and really isolate building blocks that are true precursors to the students' next learning steps.

While building learning progressions, teachers must take great care not to identify too many building blocks. In the course of instruction, it will be necessary to assess students' mastery of every building block in the learning progression, and if a progression contains lots and lots of building blocks, this sort of en route assessment becomes a lot less feasible. I urge educators who tackle the building of learning progressions to *lean toward lean*. It make gobs of instructional sense to identify two or three truly necessary building blocks, measure students' mastery of those building blocks along the way, and then make any instructional adjustments that seem warranted. Teachers aiming to measure 8 to 10 building blocks per target curricular aim are likely to find the entire enterprise prohibitively complicated and time-consuming.

Step 3: Assessing building-block mastery. The next step in creating a useful learning progression involves a determination of whether it will be possible to measure students' mastery of each identified building block. Again, fewer building blocks in a learning progression will require less en route assessment than a large number of building blocks will. But one important reason teachers build learning progressions is to monitor students' progress toward mastery of the target curricular aim. If building-block mastery cannot be assessed, then this potent payoff from a learning progression disappears.

The assessment approaches to be used in gauging students' building-block mastery need not consist of formal tests such as multiple-choice assessments or essay exams. Informal methods are often perfectly suited to the job. For instance, thinking back to the curricular aim dealing with students' use of reference tools, a teacher might ask questions about different tools' uses, then prompt students to use whiteboards to provide short answers. Similarly, a teacher could pose oral or on-the-chalkboard multiple-choice questions; signal students to hold up prepared index cards emblazoned with the letters *A, B, C,* and *D;* and then judge whether students seem to be understanding what is being taught.

Step 4: Sequencing the building blocks. Creating a learning progression entails not only identifying which subskills and bodies of enabling knowledge are essential for achieving a target curricular aim but also placing these building blocks in the most effective instructional sequence. Sometimes the most appropriate series of building blocks will be fairly obvious. Often it won't. In those more opaque situations, teachers will need to supply their best professional judgment about the ordering of subskills and enabling knowledge in a learning progression.

In a limited number of settings, substantial efforts by both government and nongovernmental agencies have generated building-block sequences and tried them out with large numbers of students. Such agencies have, thereby, identified *empirically authenticated* "effective" learning progressions. The Australian Council on Educational Research has been particularly active in this regard (Masters & Forster, 1996). If you are a teacher and any of these empirically based learning progressions happen to be available to you and happen to mesh with your own curricular aims, then you should surely consider adopting or adapting them.

Most of the time, however, teachers will generate their own learning progressions, either on their own or in collaboration with colleagues in a team-teaching situation or in a professional learning community. It's definitely worth cautioning that searching for *the* one-and-only-one "correct" set of building blocks and *the* one-and-only-one "correct" way to sequence these building blocks is a great way to squander tons of time and drive oneself mildly crazy. A learning progression is a hypothesis, built, as hypotheses are, on past knowledge, insight, wisdom, and evidence of what has worked before. Teachers should dive in, use their best judgment, and select and sequence those building blocks that they believe will lead to curricular aim mastery.

Remember, too, that because teachers need at least a rudimentary learning progression for each of their most significant curricular aims, the creation of too-fancy learning progressions can lead to teacher burnout and the abandonment of the whole enterprise. It's better to *always* create simple learning progressions for super-significant curricular aims based on truly *essential* building blocks than it is to bypass this excellent way of gaining a better understanding of a curricular aim before designing instruction because it is "too much trouble."

Many teachers, especially those who are more visually oriented, find it useful to represent learning progressions graphically, in a manner such as you see in Figure 4.3. Subskills are represented as circles, and each body of enabling knowledge is represented as a square. Finally, you'll see that a target curricular aim is depicted as a rectangle. If you wish to do so, of course, you can enter the actual names of the building blocks and target curricular aim—or at least an abbreviated version of those names.

It does take time to generate both end-of-instruction tests and carefully considered learning progression before getting into the actual design of instruction related to a significant curricular aim. It is always so tempting to "just start teaching." But a just-start-teaching approach will typically shortchange students and also diminish the teacher's chances of being instructionally successful. The better a teacher understands the nature of a curricular aim—its viscera and its nuances—the better that teacher's instructional design will be. Time spent up front in fully understanding a curricular aim will yield important instructional dividends later on.

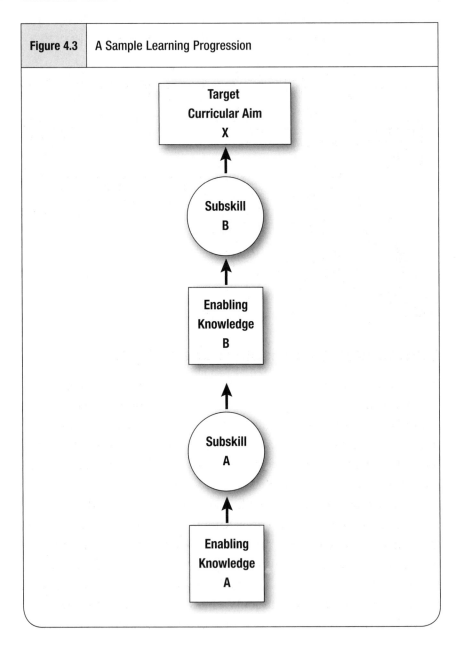

Figure 4.3 | A Sample Learning Progression

Communicate Curricular Expectations

It's said that motorists can't get the most benefit from a road map unless they know their destination. Similarly, students find it difficult to successfully learn something if they don't know what that something is. It follows that, at the outset of an instructional sequence, teachers need to let students know just what they are supposed to learn and take steps to ensure students understand those expectations.

In the 1960s and 1970s, I taught an instructional methods course for prospective teachers as part of the UCLA teacher education program. In that course I tried to dish out only a very modest number of instructional guidelines to my students. One of my few guidelines I labeled *Revelation of Objectives*. The phrase had an almost-scriptural aura, and I always enjoyed explaining to my students why it was important for teachers not only to describe their instructional objectives to students but also to help their students understand *why* such objectives were worth pursuing in the first place.

In hindsight, I now realize that revealing objectives and defending their worth is insufficient. What I should have been advocating, and what I now recommend, is that teachers clarify *fully* the nature of all significant curricular aims for their students. More specifically, at the outset of any meaningful segment of instruction, whether that be a new school term or the start of a multiweek instructional unit, teachers need to let their students know *four* things about curricular expectations:

1. The nature of the curricular aim itself
2. The evaluative criteria by which the achievement of that aim will be judged
3. What acceptable and unacceptable student performances look like
4. The most important building blocks in the curricular aim's learning progression

Because this sort of teacher-to-student communication must be provided at the beginning of an instructional sequence, it is obvious that many students won't know all that much regarding what's about to be taught. It's essential, then, that teachers provide their curricular aim explanations in grade-level-appropriate, kid-friendly lingo. But that, in itself, is not enough. Frankly, telling students who don't know something how they can tell when they *do know* that same something is far from fool's play. Let's take a closer look at how to tackle this challenge.

Explaining the Nature of the Curricular Aim

The statement of a curricular aim itself, presented in the most simple form possible, can sometimes be sufficient—but not usually. And, in passing, it is not an altogether crazy idea to let your students know why mastering this curricular aim would be advantageous to them.

In his analysis of how teachers can teach most effectively, Marzano (2007) reminds us that when teachers communicate curricular aims to their students, it is important to distinguish between curricular aims (which Marzano refers to as "learning goals") and the instructional activities in which students are to engage. As he points out, many students erroneously believe that upcoming activities or assignments are actually learning goals. For instance, suppose a science teacher's curricular aim was the following: "Students will be able to accurately display scientific evidence in two or more different data display graphs." Well, in order to help students achieve that curricular aim, the teacher might plan for students to

- Read Chapter 5 in the textbook regarding graphic and tabular displays of scientific data.
- Collect examples of graphic data displays from newspapers, popular magazines, and online publications.
- Work with a partner to create at least three different graphic ways of displaying the numerical scientific data contained in Appendix B of the textbook.

Note, though, that all of the above are activities or assignments for the future. These are things students must do in order to accomplish the curricular aim that's being sought. Students need to understand the difference between intended ends of instruction and the intended means for achieving those ends. And this is why Marzano suggests that teachers, early on, "Make a distinction between learning goals and learning activities or assignments" (2007, p. 17).

I've been advocating the use of clearly stated instructional objectives for well over four decades. In the early 1960s, for example, I spent an inordinate amount of time urging teachers to state their instructional objectives in the form of the sorts of behaviors students should be able to display at the close of an effective chunk of instruction. These statements of instructional intentions were referred to as "behavioral objectives," and I gave speeches, wrote articles, wrote books, and developed audiovisual programs touting the virtues of behaviorally stated instructional objectives. Indeed, Michael Scriven, the famous educational evaluator, once described me as "the licensed midwife to the birth of behavioral objectives in the U.S." So, pretty clearly, I have always grooved on properly stated instructional objectives (which, in my recent writing, I now refer to as "curricular aims").

Well, during the last year or two I have been almost dumbstruck to see many teachers in the United States and Canada stating what they refer to as *educational objectives* in the form of instructional activities. I suppose if you've been yammering about something for so long, you assume someone has been listening. But Marzano is absolutely correct about the need for teachers to help students see the difference between an intended curricular end (call it whatever you want) and a set of instructional activities. What worries me is that I've talked to hoards of teachers during recent years, and way too many of them do not really grasp the pivotal distinction between instructional means and curricular ends. I hope—no, I pray—that you do.

Communicating Evaluative Criteria

The evaluative criteria are the factors the teacher will use to distinguish qualitatively among their students' performances. To illustrate, if students are being asked to read a brief narrative selection intended to convey a central message and then compose a single sentence that accurately captures the selection's central message, the following evaluative criteria might be employed to judge the quality of the student's "central message statement":

- *Accuracy.* The central message statement must be a correct representation of the narrative selection's central message.
- *Suitable scope.* The central message statement must be neither too broad nor too narrow but must instead reflect the breadth of the central message in the narrative selection.
- *Appropriate but original language.* The central message statement must be well-chosen without repeating the exact vocabulary employed in the narrative selection.

Students who understand that the main idea statements they compose must be accurate, be of suitable scope, and employ appropriate but original language are more likely to generate acceptable main idea statements than will students who are unaware of these three evaluative criteria.

Although a rubric (or scoring guide) is often created to assist in the end-of-instruction judging of students' performances on constructed-response items, rubrics can be enormously helpful during instruction itself. Indeed, the evaluative criteria set forth in a rubric can be particularly helpful, even when students encounter selected-response items. Think about it: If students' ability to discern a narrative passage's central message were to be assessed with multiple-choice items, then the three evaluative criteria I've identified—accuracy, suitable scope, and appropriate but original language—will surely play a prominent role in determining correct and incorrect answer-choices for such items.

As students begin to increase their command of what's being taught, their awareness of the evaluative factors to be used in judging their performances can be a potent force in shaping the way those students are learning. A well-crafted rubric gives students a template for judging the adequacy of their own performances, both now and in the future.

Providing Illustrative Student Performances

Next, we come to the exemplars of strong and weak performances. Furnishing these can be a matter of distributing copies of excellent and subpar work from past students (with the names removed, naturally). If no such responses are available, then teachers can simply create several illustrative responses themselves (telling students, of course, that these were teacher generated, not actual student-generated illustrative responses).

Because most students will be unfamiliar with the skill or knowledge with which they're dealing, teachers should distribute illustrative work in which the quality differences are striking rather than subtle. Teachers might even highlight the key factors that make these pieces wonderful or woeful. When instruction is further along, students may be able to detect nuanced differences in response quality. At the beginning of instruction, however, a teacher is merely trying to help students get a general idea of what's expected of them and how to distinguish between acceptable and unacceptable responses.

Sharing and Explaining the Learning Progression

Students benefit not just from knowing where they're headed instructionally but also from having at least a rough idea about how they're supposed to get there. As soon as a teacher senses students have grasped the essence of the curricular aim being sought, the teacher should let students know at least the most important of the building blocks in the learning progression devised for that curricular aim. Sometimes, especially if a teacher has constructed a lean learning progression with just a few building blocks, what the teacher might end up describing to students is the learning progression in its entirety.

For example, suppose you were a middle school social studies teacher and wanted your students to be able to create outlines to organize complex content. Your target curricular aim for a two-week unit on outlining might be something along these lines: "Students will be able to generate original outlines that accurately but succinctly represent a complex body of social studies content." As you work up a learning progression underlying this skill, you might conclude that there are only two building blocks in this progression, and they are ordered as follows:

1. Students must know the standard conventions of outlining, including the way that letters, numbers, and indentation are employed for certain major and minor categories.

2. Students must be able to conceptualize defensible ways of organizing complex content into categories that either subsume or contribute to other categories.

Figure 4.4 shows how this two-building-block learning progression can be depicted graphically. Note that it is displayed horizontally, in contrast to Figure 4.3's vertical set-up. Learning progression orientation is a matter of personal preference.

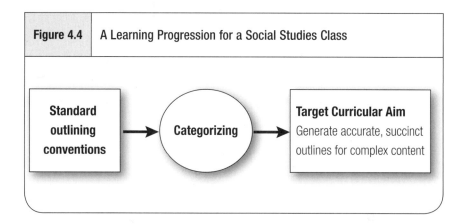

Figure 4.4 | A Learning Progression for a Social Studies Class

Standard outlining conventions → Categorizing → Target Curricular Aim: Generate accurate, succinct outlines for complex content

Now, if you, as a middle school teacher, were trying to communicate this short learning progression to your students, you could display this learning progression and leave it posted for students to consult. Then, you might describe both building blocks, the first one being a body of enabling knowledge and the second one being a subskill. After that, you might provide an example or two of both building blocks. What you would be trying to get your students to understand is the nature of the target curricular aim as well as the two chief stepping stones you think they must master to achieve that aim. The better that students understand what they must do to master a target curricular aim, the more focused those students' learning activities typically will be.

One Exception: Keeping Affective Curricular Aims Under Wraps

You will know by now that I encourage the routine pursuit of curricular aims dealing with students' affect—their attitudes, interests, and values. Teachers who decide to do this definitely need to attend to students' affect when designing instructional plans. However, teachers who decide to promote an affective curricular aim should not reveal this affective goal to their students—ever.

As noted in Chapter 2, the best way for teachers to assess students' affect is by using anonymous, self-report inventories. For such inventories to provide a teacher with sufficiently accurate information about a student *group's* affect, the bulk of those students need to respond honestly to the items on these self-report inventories. Realistically, if students recognize what sorts of affective goals the teacher is pursuing, there's too much likelihood they will supply "socially desirable" responses—that is, responses they believe the teacher wants them to make. If a teacher simply doesn't communicate the nature of any affective aims to students, the odds of getting honest answers increase.

Identify Time-on-Task Activities

One of the last century's more powerful research-based conclusions regarding instruction was that sufficient *engaged time on task* is pivotal to instructional success. Students will learn better if they have plenty of opportunity to practice what they're supposed to be learning. Oversimplifying by a bit, but not by much, the notion that "practice makes perfect" is not only alluringly alliterative but also solidly supported by empirical research. See, for example, the review of practice-related research in Chapter 3 of Marzano's *The Art and Science of Teaching* (2007).

What the advocacy of students' engaged time on task means for instructional design is straightforward. If the curricular aim involved calls for a teacher's students to acquire a high-level cognitive skill, such as being able to evaluate the cogency of newspaper editorials, then during the instruction intended to promote their mastery of that skill, those students must get plenty of practice applying this particular high-level cognitive skill. However, a student's mastery of a truly challenging curricular aim is often dependent on mastery of key cognitive subskills and bodies of enabling knowledge. My recommendation, then, is for teachers to install ample opportunities for students to practice using the skill or knowledge represented by a curricular aim *and* to practice each of the building blocks in a curricular aim's learning progression. So, for example, if a teacher's target curricular aim is to get students to be able to evaluate the cogency of newspaper articles, a learning progression for this skill might contain only two subskills: (1) being able to determine the accuracy of an editorial's content and (2) judging the adequacy of the editorial's logic. The teacher, in view of this learning progression, should give students guided and independent practice on both building blocks and on the target curricular aim's ultimate skill.

Earlier, I recommended that teachers create their end-of-instruction assessments prior to their instructional design decisions as a way to gain a better understanding of the nature of the curricular aim being pursued. It should come as no surprise, therefore, that I think teachers should at least *think through* the nature of the assessments they can use to verify whether their students have mastered each of the major building blocks in a learning progression. Ideally, teachers should actually create those assessments because they'll want to use them, later on, as a pivotal part of the formative assessment process. And, of course, the act of using assessments to exemplify each subskill or body of enabling knowledge in a learning progression helps the teacher gain better insight into the nature of those building blocks.

Engaging Students in Time-on-Task Activities

How do teachers get their students to engage in time on task? Well, this certainly depends on the students the teacher has and the curricular aims the teacher is pursuing. But Figure 4.5 depicts a four-step procedure that will usually work quite well. It calls for teachers to provide their students with (1) *explanation,* (2) *modeling,* (3) *guided practice,* and (4) *independent practice.* Let's briefly consider each of these four steps.

Step 1: Explanation. For most curricular aims, students will require explanations. For example, suppose (as a curricular aim), a teacher wanted students to be able to critique the quality of their own oral presentations by using a rubric containing four evaluative criteria. The teacher would begin by explaining to the students—perhaps in lecture format—the meaning of the rubric's four evaluative factors and how to apply those factors to the judging of oral communication. Such explanations might also be found in students' textbooks or in other assigned readings.

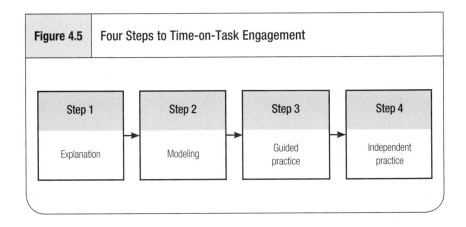

Figure 4.5   Four Steps to Time-on-Task Engagement

Step 1	Step 2	Step 3	Step 4
Explanation	Modeling	Guided practice	Independent practice

Step 2: Modeling. It's often helpful for students to see "what it would look like" to actually have mastered the curricular aim. In many instances, the teacher will have provided this sort of modeling earlier in the instructional sequence, while communicating curricular expectations (see p. 85). However, at this stage, it is typically beneficial to students if they can see someone (not necessarily the teacher) model the successful usage of the skill, subskill, or knowledge being sought.

Step 3: Guided practice. The more demanding a curricular aim is, the greater the likelihood that students will need assistance as they begin to use the skill or body of knowledge it represents. Thus, as a teacher designs instructional activities revolving around students' practice, the teacher should be certain to build in ways she (or several of her more advanced students) might steer students toward appropriate practice. Ideally, as students become more adept in using a skill or a body of knowledge, they can monitor the quality of their own performance, referring to teacher-supplied answer keys or rubrics. During the early stages of most time-on-task sequences, however, teachers must be ready to give students plenty of improvement-oriented guidance.

Step 4: Independent practice. Here's the point at which students are supposed to "fly solo," that is, without guidance from the teacher or from peers, as they display genuine mastery of what's present in a curricular aim. This is the phase of instruction when the research evidence supporting engaged time on task is especially germane. Independent practice is a truly critical component of almost any successful instructional design, as it helps ensure that students' mastery of the sought-for skill or knowledge will be deeply engrained rather than superficially acquired.

Deciding on Practice Types and Amounts

Engaged time on task is a crucial component of almost any instructional sequence, but teachers also need to consider two related issues.

What type of practice? If a teacher regards a curricular aim as sufficiently important to pursue instructionally, the teacher obviously wants students to master that aim and master it well. This almost always means that teachers want their students to demonstrate mastery of the curricular aim in a *generalizable* manner. A teacher should not want students to be able to display mastery of a skill *only* in the particular way the teacher has chosen to measure their skill mastery.

To illustrate, let's say you're a teacher and the accountability test you will administer to your students calls for them to display mastery of a "main idea" comprehension skill by first reading a paragraph containing either an explicitly stated or readily inferable main idea, then selecting a reasonable statement of that main idea from a set of multiple-choice options. Obviously, you ought to give your students plenty of practice discerning main ideas by employing the sorts of multiple-choice items the accountability test will use. However, to promote students' *generalizable* mastery of this important reading skill, you should also have your students take part in time-on-task activities in which they must *generate* their own statements of a paragraph's main idea, both orally and in writing.

We want students to master skills deeply so that they can apply those skills in a variety of settings, not only in response to a single species of test item. Consequently, teachers should be sure the guided or independent practice opportunities they give their students represent a *range* of ways to display students' generalizable mastery of a curricular aim. There's a simple way for teachers to verify that their students are learning things in generalizable ways. If you're a teacher, just dream up a variety of ways to assess students' learning, then ask yourself this question: *Based on how I am currently teaching my students, will they be able to respond correctly to the full kit and caboodle of my imagined testing techniques?* If you can supply an affirmative answer, you are doing fine.

How much practice? This is a question for which, if there were enough classroom time available, an appropriate response might be "The more practice time, the better!" But these days, with so much to be taught, and with so much of what's taught to be assessed via external accountability tests, most teachers simply don't have enough classroom time to provide lengthy, languorous time-on-task sessions for their students.

What teachers need to aim for is a number of time-on-task activities sufficient to help students master a curricular aim deeply, but not so many that teachers are unable to pursue other worthwhile educational goals. Fortunately, as we'll see in the next and final instructional design recommendation, this is an instance when teachers can use students' performances on their classroom tests to help them answer the "how much" question. Teachers can bolster their judgments about how much engaged time on task they need by relying on en route assessment evidence regarding their students' current performance levels.

Identify Occasions for Formative Assessment Decisions

Formative assessment, as explained in Chapter 2, is the process of using assessment-elicited evidence from students to supply progress-related feedback to a teacher or to the students themselves. It is intended to supply the sort of evidence permitting (1) teachers to adjust how they're teaching or (2) students to adjust how they're trying to learn something. In the research review of classroom formative assessment by Black and Wiliam (1998a), the positive correlation between student learning and teachers' employment of formative assessment testifies to the likely effectiveness of the process. Of course, formative assessment can be effective only if teachers use it; hence, my final instructional design recommendation is for teachers to identify sufficient occasions to collect the evidence needed for formative assessment.

This recommendation is intended to caution teachers to avoid the all-too-common tendency to design instruction with an exclusive focus on *teaching* and, thus, neglect teaching's ultimate purpose: students' *learning*. The function of formative assessment is to improve learning by helping teachers and their students decide whether any adjustments are needed during a lesson or series of lessons. In Chapter 5, we'll look closer at the *when* and *how* of formative assessment, but the key idea here is that teachers must routinely *plan* to incorporate time for formative assessment evidence gathering at appropriate junctures in their lessons—those junctures at which adjustments in instructional tactics or learning tactics are likely to be most beneficial. Here, learning progressions, indicating the subskills and bodies of enabling knowledge necessary to master the curricular aim being sought, provide valuable illumination.

To illustrate, if a teacher's task analysis reveals that there appear to be three pivotal subskills a student needs to have mastered prior to achieving a more distant curricular aim, that teacher could build a multiple-choice assessment instrument with items focused on each of the resultant learning progression's three subskills. After students had completed such an assessment, the teacher would be able identify if a particular student were having difficulty with one or more of the three subskills. (One obvious way to pinpoint the nature of students' difficulties via a multiple-choice quiz would be to construct each item's wrong-answer options so they arise from a specific, instructionally addressable misunderstanding.) If a teacher constructs such an assessment *without* deliberately incorporating sufficient per-subskill items, he would miss an opportunity to help identify *where* students are having problems in their learning.

Remembering that formative assessment is a process rather than a particular kind of test, and that informal sorts of evidence-gathering procedures can often supply the needed evidence for feedback, the underlying idea associated with this final instructional design recommendation is that teachers need to incorporate evidence-collecting procedures (both formal and informal) into their lessons so they and their students obtain information indicating whether any adjustments are needed. If more than a week goes by without some form of formatively-focused assessment taking place in the classroom, those teachers are probably supplying insufficient feedback to their students—and to themselves.

Considering only the payoff of formative assessment to teachers, the more frequently a teacher can elicit evidence of student progress, the more information the teacher will have at hand to tell whether any instructional adjustments are warranted and, if so, what kind of adjustments are advisable. A successful teacher is one who can adapt with agility to the ever-changing and often unpredictable nature of students' progress. But, agility notwithstanding, instructional adjustments based on whim are rarely successful. Frequent assessment of students' progress provides feedback so teachers' instructional adjustments, and their students' learning tactic adjustments, can be rooted in reality.

✔ Chapter Check-Back

- To acquire a thorough understanding of each of their important curricular aims, teachers should create end-of-instruction assessments as the first step in their instructional design process and develop a learning progression for their most significant curricular aims.
- Teachers should communicate curricular expectations to students by describing each curricular aim, citing the evaluative criteria associated with that aim, supplying examples of student performances that are acceptable and unacceptable, and explaining the key elements of a curricular aim's learning progression.
- Teachers must provide students with sufficient time-on-task activities that are related not only to a curricular aim itself but also to any of the aim's important subskills and bodies of enabling knowledge.
- Teachers must be sure to incorporate ample occasions for the formative assessment process in all instructional designs.

Suggestions for Further Reading

Marzano, R. J. (2007). *The art and science of teaching: A comprehensive framework for effective teaching.* Alexandria, VA: ASCD.

It's difficult to think of a book that's more relevant to the instructional focus of this chapter than Marzano's highly readable analysis of how teachers can tackle instructional design. By laying out his framework in the form of 10 practical questions (such as "What will I do to engage students?"), he gives teachers a set of classroom realities to consider. If his 10 questions had been commandments, stone tablets would be in order. This is a book well worth a teacher's reading time.

Marzano, R. J., Pickering, D. J., & Pollock, J. E. (2001). *Classroom instruction that works: Research-based strategies for increasing student achievement.* Alexandria, VA: ASCD.

Anytime a million copies of an education-related book have been sold, you'd have to conclude the book must have something going for it other than a clever cover. Well, that's definitely the case for this modern-day classic, in which Marzano, Pickering, and Pollock coalesce decades of educational research into a readable array of nine instructional strategies likely to maximize students' achievement.

Serdyukov, P., & Ryan, M. (2008). *Writing effective lesson plans: A 5-star approach.* Boston: Allyn & Bacon.

In this theory-based but highly practical treatment of lesson planning, readers learn about how to effectively design instruction. The book, written for both experienced and beginning teachers, also addresses the most common obstacles faced when designing lesson plans.

Wiggins, G., & McTighe, J. (2005). *Understanding by design* (2nd ed.). Alexandria, VA: ASCD.

Since the introduction of Understanding by Design (UbD) in 1998, thousands of educators around the world have structured their instructional planning on this three-stage strategy, which is consonant with an assessment-influenced approach. UbD calls for teachers to (1) identify a desired result in students, (2) determine acceptable evidence of results, and, only then, move on to (3) plan learning experiences and instruction. In this expanded second edition, Wiggins and McTighe have sharpened and tightened what was already a first-rate way of thinking about the design of instruction.

5

Monitoring Instruction and Learning

If you are or once were a teacher, you can probably remember being in the midst of a particular lesson and being certain that what you were doing was working. You just knew your students were learning what you were trying to teach them. Probably you can also remember a time when you sensed your instruction was bombing. Indeed, most teachers can arrive at reasonably accurate judgments about the quality of their instruction while it's taking place, as long as that instruction is *extraordinarily good* or *extraordinarily bad*. Of course, the vast majority of day-in and day-out instruction falls somewhere between those two extremes. Accordingly, in this chapter we'll be looking at more reliable ways that teachers can monitor their own instruction and its effectiveness in promoting student learning.

The means I recommend is formative assessment, which, as we've established, is a process in which teachers gather ongoing, assessment-elicited evidence that they can use to make any necessary adjustments in how they're teaching, and that their students can use to make any necessary adjustments in how they're learning. To some educators, the idea that assessment should play such a pivotal role in instruction may seem counterintuitive. However, as Dylan Wiliam, a leading British assessment expert, observed

> Assessment is the key process in instruction. It is only through assessment that we can find out whether what has been taught has been learned. Assessment is, therefore, the bridge between teaching and learning. (Personal communication, November 7, 2006)

The middle sentence in this three-sentence quotation is one I'd like to see in neon lights above the entrance to every school in the world. Educators should never be allowed to forget that *it is only through assessment that we can find out whether what has been taught has been learned.* Accordingly, that's why I have organized this chapter on monitoring instruction around the role that formative assessment can play in helping both teachers and students find out what's actually transpiring during instruction.

Schematically, then, monitoring of ongoing instruction ends up with the dual focus depicted in Figure 5.1. As you can see, the process of formative assessment can supply the evidence it elicits to either the teacher or the teacher's students. Although often the same assessment activities will provide valuable evidence for both teachers *and* students, sometimes the information needs of teachers and students are sufficiently distinctive to call for meaningfully different formative assessment procedures.

The information needs of both these groups merits discussion. Let's begin by focusing on the teachers: the kind of information that will help them monitor their instruction and their students' learning, as well as some of the means they can use to acquire this information.

Teachers' En Route Information Needs

From a teacher's perspective, the monitoring of ongoing instruction has one overriding purpose: to make instruction better in order to enhance students' learning. Making instruction better rests on two key decisions: (1) teachers' deciding if they need to change what they are currently doing and, thereafter, (2) teachers' deciding what sort of changes need to be made.

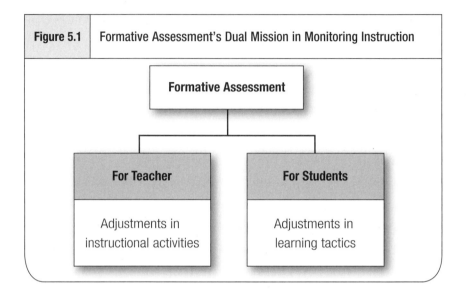

Figure 5.1   Formative Assessment's Dual Mission in Monitoring Instruction

Formative Assessment

For Teacher

Adjustments in instructional activities

For Students

Adjustments in learning tactics

While we're making numerical lists, I'll add that the decisions teachers might make about adjusting their ongoing instruction can be conveniently classified into three categories: (1) intra-lesson adjustments, (2) next-lesson adjustments, and (3) multi-lesson adjustments. Note that by *lesson,* I mean a day's worth of instruction for a given group of students, typically focused on one curricular aim in a particular content area.

A simple example of an *intra-lesson adjustment* is when the teacher decides to spend an extra, unplanned 15 minutes on the promotion of a specific subskill necessary to achieve a more distant curricular aim. *Next-lesson adjustments* are the changes a teacher makes when the need to alter instructional activities planned for the subsequent day's lesson is apparent. The most common reason for a next-lesson adjustment is that students seem to be struggling with what the teacher thought would be an easily comprehended concept. Finally, *multi-lesson adjustments* involve two or more upcoming lessons. An example might be when a teacher discovers, in the first week of a three-week unit, that students already possess some key enabling knowledge intended to be the focus of two lessons in the third week of instruction. Because students already know what the teacher was planning to teach during that pair of lessons, there will be no need to devote instructional time to this material.

Answering the Two Key Questions for Instructional Monitoring

Whether a teacher's instructional-monitoring decisions relate to an in-progress lesson, a lesson that's scheduled next, or a flock of subsequent lessons, those decisions will always boil down to how the teacher answers the following two questions:

1. *The Whether Question:* Do I need to make any adjustments?
2. *The What Question:* If I do need to make any adjustments, what should those adjustments be?

The asking and answering of these questions are key to high-quality, effective instruction.

For centuries, almost all teachers have been making *whether* and *what* decisions regarding their in-progress instruction, but usually they have based these decisions on intuitive judgment. Today, we have substantial evidence indicating that teachers can come up with far better answers to the whether-to-adjust and the what-to-adjust questions if they inform their adjustment decisions using evidence yielded from formative assessment. Will *all* of a teacher's assessment-based decisions about instructional adjustments be correct and *all* of that teacher's intuition-based decisions about instructional adjustments be wrong? Of course not. However, the odds of teachers making *appropriate* adjustment decisions will be much greater if teachers incorporate assessment evidence into their adjustment-decision deliberations.

Decision occasions. How often in the course of instruction should teachers gather assessment evidence for the purpose of making en route adjustment decisions? The learning progression generated during the instructional planning phase provides an excellent map to the key assessment points and, thus, to the necessary decision occasions. While teachers certainly may collect assessment evidence at other points—both through formal means (like tests, quizzes, and assignments) and informal means (like classroom discussions and Q&A sessions), it's the building blocks that provide the essential guide to what students must master. This is why, as noted in Chapter 4, teachers ought to keep their own assessment tolerance in mind when they are crafting learning progressions. It makes no sense to gather more evidence that you're prepared to consider, and setting too aggressive a slate of en route evidence gathering is the quickest way to burn out on the whole idea and lose all the extraordinary benefits formative assessment can bring.

The *whether-to-adjust* decision. When assessment evidence suggests that many or most students have not mastered a building block, the teacher's conclusion should be clear: *It's adjustment time!* However, the answer to the *whether* question will not always be so obvious. Accordingly, teachers need to determine what would make the case for and against adjustment. This means looking at each of a progression's building blocks and deciding what level of student performance on a building block would persuade them to adjust their instruction and what level of student performance on a building block would persuade them *not* to adjust their instruction.

Ultimately, every adjust-or-not-adjust decision should be made on the basis of this kind of predetermined *adjustment trigger* for the building block in question. Each adjustment trigger has two components:

1. A *per-student performance level,* which indicates how well an individual student must perform in order for the teacher to be confident that there's no need for instructional adjustment.

2. A *per-class performance level,* which indicates what proportion of the class must perform satisfactorily (at the per-student performance level) in order for the teacher to be confident that there's no need for instructional adjustment.

A teacher might articulate an adjustment trigger like this:

Per-student performance level: To signify adequate mastery of Building Block 2, a student must answer at least 8 items correctly on the 10-item quiz created to assess that building block.

Per-class performance level: I will not need to make any instructional adjustments related to Building Block 2 if at least 90 percent of my students equal or exceed the per-student performance level I have set.

For teachers, the chief advantage of establishing adjustment triggers for every adjustment occasion *before* administering an assessment is that it helps defend against "good enoughness"—the conclusion that students' performances on a building-block assessment might not be great but are "good enough," and that instruction can proceed without alteration. Today's time-pressed teachers can be particularly vulnerable to this affliction. Sure, teachers can sometimes make mistakes when they establish assessment triggers, perhaps setting the per-student performance level too low (and, thus, not making an adjustment when one is needed), or perhaps establishing a per-class performance level that is a little too high (and, thus, altering instruction that was working pretty well for most students). However, making a specific, best-judgment determination of how well students should perform on the assessment of each building bock is still the most reasonable, *practical* way to approach the whether-to-adjust question.

I want to note specifically there's no rule stating that teachers must make en route instructional adjustments and no pedagogical precept saying that a teacher can't get a lesson right the first time. Teachers who come up with a "no need" answer to the whether-to-adjust question should take a few mental bows for their well-designed instruction. Those teachers who *do* get the "need to adjust" answer should simply move on to the next question—and the next critical decision.

The *what-to-adjust* decision. Gathering assessment-elicited evidence relative to a what-to-adjust decision is a more vexing issue than it might seem. For each building block in a learning progression, it's certainly possible to design an adjust-or-don't-adjust assessment incorporating items that will also illuminate what aspects of instruction might be adjusted. However, teachers should bear in mind that if their assessment returns evidence supporting a no-adjustment-needed conclusion, the amount of time it took students to respond to the items dealing with the *what-to-adjust* question will have been time wasted. For this reason, I recommend teachers use a second assessment to get an indication of what to adjust, and administer it only after deciding that adjustment really is warranted. This is an approach that's more respectful of students' time and of teachers' time, as well.

Getting the Information Needed: Assessment Procedures

Let's look now at some of the assessment procedures teachers might use to monitor their instruction and their students' learning. Properly deployed, all of these will generate evidence of students' covert status—the information teachers need to make the key decisions we've just considered. And all of these procedures can and should be tailored to the particulars of teachers' own teaching styles, their curricular aims, their students, and so on.

Class discussions or Q&A sessions. One of the most efficient ways for teachers to get a fix on students' status with respect to any building block is to carry out a structured classroom discussion or question-and-answer session. Typically, these sorts of total-class activities will take place after a teacher has explained a concept or after students have completed a reading assignment—possibly as homework. As Leahy and her colleagues (2005) note, *well-engineered* classroom discussions and Q&A sessions are a formative assessment approach that is "powerful for teachers of all content areas and at all grade levels" (p. 20).

To help ensure that a classroom discussion will generate the sort of adjustment-decision evidence necessary for formative assessment, teachers should plan to ask one or more questions *deliberately designed* to yield the information that will factor into their adjustment decision. There are a couple of ways to approach this evidence gathering.

All-student responses. Because the goal here is to gauge the status of the entire class rather than the status of one or two particularly vocal students, teachers must be sure to elicit *all-student* responses to these questions as opposed to *single-student* responses. Two procedures are particularly effective here: *letter cards* and *whiteboard short answers.*

In the *letter card* technique, the teacher posts a key selected-response question for the entire class to see—perhaps writing it on the chalkboard or projecting in on a screen. At the teacher's cue, students hold up *letter cards* (for example, five- by seven-inch index cards indicating A, B, C, or D) so that only the teacher can see the students' responses. If the correct answer is Choice A, but the teacher finds more than half the class is opting for Choice D, this is pretty compelling evidence supporting an adjustment decision. The teacher ought also to address the content represented by wrong-answer Choice D posthaste. An on-the-spot explanation of why Choice D is all wrong may be sufficient, or a more elaborate treatment of it may be required. Similar all-student response procedures can be employed for binary-choice questions: T and F cards, for example, for True/False items. Many teachers also provide students with question mark cards so that students can signify uncertainty rather than guess (sometimes wildly).

Teachers who wish to incorporate short, constructed-response questions in their Q&A session or group discussions can do so by distributing a small, erasable whiteboard and marking pen to everyone in the class. Each student responds to the teacher's posted, constructed-response question by writing a short answer—a word or a phrase—on his or her whiteboard. Then, at the teacher's signal, all students raise their whiteboard responses for the teacher to see. Note that the success of both these all-student response procedures depends on the teacher's clarifying how students should display their answers.

Random-respondent procedures. In traditional classroom questioning, the teacher asks a question and then calls on a volunteer to provide the answer. With *random-respondent procedures,* any student may be called on to respond to a question, and this eligibility tends to raise student alertness levels and increase cognitive engagement. One such procedure involves the teacher's keeping a collection of wooden tongue depressors, each of which is labeled with a student's name. At points throughout the lesson, the teacher draws a tongue depressor from the collection's container and asks that student to respond to a question. Another option would be to assign each student a number and then use an actual table of random numbers (found in the appendix of most statistics textbooks) to select the "chosen" answerer.

Random-respondent procedures, though effective for keeping students actively engaged in a lesson, are *not* suitable as a standalone way to gather evidence for adjustment decisions, which should be made on the basis of how all students (or at least almost all students) are doing, not just how a few, randomly selected students are doing. Teachers who employ random-respondent procedures as part of formative assessment should always supplement them with all-student response procedures, such as the use of letter cards or whiteboards.

Student self-status procedures. These assessment measures involve a teacher prompting students to signal their own level of understanding, after which the teacher decides, based on previously chosen adjustment triggers, whether any instructional adjustments are warranted. Two easy-to-use examples are the *traffic signal* procedure and the *thumb signals* procedure.

Traffic signal procedure. This technique, which requires a bit of advance preparation and explanation, can be employed on a continuous basis or periodically, as it suits the teacher. Here, the teacher provides all students with a set of three colored plastic or paper drinking cups: one red, one yellow, and one green. (Colored three- by five-inch cards can also be used, but they're tougher for teachers to see.) Students keep their set of cups on their desk, upside down and in a stack, with the red cup on the bottom, the yellow cup on top of the red, and the green cup on top of the yellow. The teacher explains that each student is to leave the green cup visible on top of the cup stack if he or she understands what's being taught *well enough to explain it to other students.* A student moves the yellow cup to the top of the stack if he or she is somewhat uncertain about what's being treated. The red cup gets placed on top if the student really doesn't understand what's going on. For the teacher, the color patterns that emerge during the lesson provide an overall sense of student understanding. The idea is to decide, based on the number of yellow and red cups that appear at particular points of the lesson, whether an instructional adjustment is necessary. Most teachers who employ the traffic signal procedure have a pre-set adjustment trigger in mind, such as seeing a third or more of the students displaying yellow or red cups.

Like random-respondent procedures, the traffic signal procedure tends to foster engagement in a lesson. A teacher seeing a certain number of red cups should occasionally initiate a revised treatment of the topic under consideration by asking a "green-cup" student to explain what's going on to the rest of the class. Green-cuppers will soon appreciate the need to stay alert by discovering that they can't—and shouldn't—hide behind feigned green-cup comprehension. Yellow-cuppers should be asked to describe what parts of the lesson seem confusing. Red-cuppers should be prompted to indicate what they find perplexing.

Thumb signals. Yes, this technique consists simply of the teacher's pausing during discussion or a presentation and asking students to make either a thumbs-up signal ("I understand") or a thumbs-down signal ("I don't understand") under their chins, so that only the teacher can see. Basic as this technique is, thumb signals can be very helpful, particularly for teachers presenting complicated, multi-step procedures where the next step is dependent on a solid understanding of the preceding one.

Short-duration tests. Assessment, even when it's used for formative purposes, definitely cuts into teaching time. One way for teachers to maintain an appropriate teaching-to-testing ratio is to rely heavily on terse tests that take only a little time to complete. For example, a five-item multiple-choice test or an eight-item True/False test might supply both teachers and students with the evidence they need in order to make a whether-to-adjust decision. Short-duration tests, whether you call them *quizzes, mini-tests, testlets,* or some synonymous label, are especially useful for making decisions about intra-lesson or next-lesson adjustments. Their brevity makes them fast to design, deliver, and review, which helps to facilitate rapid adjustment of instructional approaches.

Here are a couple of examples. Imagine you're teaching a social studies lesson focused on distinguishing between statements of fact and statements of opinion in political discourse—something you have identified as a building-block subskill that's essential to students' mastery of political analysis, which is one of your long-term curricular aims. At this particular moment, you have reached the halfway point of the lesson. You have one other instructional tactic planned—an unusual peer-teaching activity—but it's something you've intended to use only if a significant number of your students are still confused about facts and opinions. So, with 25 minutes left in the class period, you dispense a brief selected-response quiz containing four political statements, two statements of fact and two statements of opinion. For each statement, a student must circle an *F* (for fact), an *O* (for opinion), or an *NS* (for not sure). You've decided on an adjustment trigger such that if one-fourth or more of your students don't answer all four items correctly, you'll definitely use the peer-teaching activity you have in reserve.

Next, students swap tests and wait for your cue. You go through the quiz, item by item, and ask for a show of hands (by the quiz-scorers, not by the quiz-takers) for the numbers of *F, O,* and *NS* responses. Within seconds, you have the information you need to make your adjustment decision: Consider the subskill as having been mastered, or proceed to the peer-teaching activity. You need not tell your students what you are doing with this formative assessment, but it's generally a good idea to do so. Teaching needn't be a mystery to the students being taught.

Let's move now to an example of how a short-duration test serves next-lesson adjustments. You're a teacher who knows what you'll be addressing in class tomorrow, but you also realize the success of tomorrow's lesson will depend on whether your students have learned the meaning of a set of nine key terms that will figure prominently in your explanation and the activities you have planned. To check students' understanding of these critical terms, you close out today's lesson with a short-answer test designed to be completed in just five minutes. The key to the test's brevity? *Item sampling.* You design three different versions of the test, each containing just three terms for which the students are to write definitions without consulting their notes or one another. Because all three test forms contain different terms to be defined, you will be getting a reasonable estimate (based on three 33-percent samples of your students) of how well your entire class understands the nine terms.

If students' scores indicate they know the key terms at the satisfactory level articulated in whatever adjustment trigger you've decided to use, you won't need to alter tomorrow's planned lesson. If students' scores fall below that level, you'll need to revise your next lesson's plans to incorporate additional vocabulary instruction, delivered via a new instructional approach.

Individual interviews. Truly differentiated instruction, as explored in the work of Carol Ann Tomlinson (2001), is a laudable goal but tough to pull off. Seasoned teachers know there's only so much time available for them to individualize their instruction and provide particular instructional activities for particular students. But, insofar as teachers have time for any one-on-one instruction, solo interviews are a terrific way to gain insight into students' status relative to the mastery of a target curricular aim and its building-block subskills and enabling knowledge.

The clear advantage of such one-on-one interviews is that a teacher can probe and follow up on student responses as the teacher sees fit. Practicality argues for keeping these interviews reasonably short because the less time it takes to conduct each one-on-one interview, the more one-on-one interviews can be completed overall. And, of course, teachers carrying out one-on-one formative interviews will need to have instructionally useful activities—such as subgroup work, silent reading, or library research—set up for the rest of the class.

Longer-duration tests. For all my championing of quickly designed and deployed assessment measures, longer-durations tests, such as performance tests, definitely have a place in the formative assessment process. Not only are they valuable ways to generate evidence for next-lesson and multi-lesson decision making, but they can also accommodate a sufficient number of items to support both teachers' whether-to-adjust decisions and their what-to-adjust decisions.

One very helpful measurement technique to employ near the end of a learning progression is a "dress rehearsal" assessment similar in form and design to the assessment the teacher will use at the conclusion of instruction. To illustrate, let's say you're a teacher who has devoted four weeks worth of lessons to the significant curricular aim of improving students' narrative composition skills. At the end of the third week of this four-week unit, you might set up a performance task in which your students will spend two days creating a narrative composition in response to a prompt you supply. On the first day, your students prewrite, plan, and organize their essays, and compose a first draft. On the second day, they revise their work and submit final narrative essays, which you read and evaluate, based on a five-point rubric where five points go to an enthralling essay and one point goes to an inept essay.

Based on your overnight (or weekend) analysis of these essays, you'll be able to snare some powerful insights about students' current status related to mastery of the ultimate curricular aim and then look to your adjustment trigger (perhaps, *If less than 80 percent of my students' essays earn four or five points on the dress rehearsal exam, an instructional adjustment is warranted*) to guide your next step: Will you proceed, as originally planned, with the final week of the four-week composition unit, or will you make some serious adjustments to your instruction during the unit's final week? You might even decide that it will take more than one additional week for your students to satisfactorily conquer narrative writing.

Longer-duration tests, especially when used as part of the formative assessment process, can be a particularly helpful tool for addressing the what-to-adjust question. On a performance test, like the narrative essay writing "dress rehearsal" just described, a teacher might employ an *analytic rubric* to get a fine-grained, potentially diagnostic picture of each student's performance, and then adjust instruction to zoom in on the analytically identified weaknesses students have displayed: addressing not just "narrative essay organization," for example, but particular components of narrative essay organization, such as maintaining a logical time sequence and using effective transitions. As another example, a teacher using a longer selected-response test during formative assessment would be able to include several items dealing with different aspects of a complex concept such as "the key requirements to be satisfied in carrying out a sound scientific experiment." By having a cluster of items dealing with each of these requirements, the teacher could get a better fix on which requirements might be causing trouble for students.

Making an Adjustment

If the initial assessment—be it a brief in-class quiz, a focused assignment, or any other of the just-considered means of eliciting students' status with respect to a building block—reveals that students haven't mastered a building block and that an instructional adjustment is necessary, teachers need to think through why their original instructional design has gone haywire. This often entails first identifying several possible reasons why students aren't getting it and then putting together a brief assessment to try to get a better fix on the specific causes of confusion. When the cause is clearer, the course of action for adjustments is usually clearer, too.

A colleague and friend, Margaret Heritage of UCLA, spends much of her time working with teachers who are attempting to employ the formative assessment process so it really pays off for students. Margaret and I often discuss parts of the formative assessment enterprise that seem to pose particular difficulties for today's teachers. We both agree that one of the most challenging tasks for teachers is to figure out what sorts of adjustments to make once it's apparent that an instructional adjustment is warranted.

Self-reflection is a teacher's ally. Throughout my entire teaching career, when my instructional approaches sputtered, it was almost always because I had failed to include sufficient time-on-task practice opportunities for my students. After I finally realized that this was my usual way to mess up instruction, I was often able to rectify an ineffective instructional sequence by sprinkling it with much more guided and independent practice. But teachers differ. If you are a teacher, perhaps you've discovered your own tendencies that get in the way of stellar instruction and have a set of go-to instructional adjustments at the ready. If you haven't, consider asking yourself the collection of questions that follow:

• *Did I omit any truly required building blocks in the learning progression I devised for this curricular aim?* If, in reconsidering a learning progression, you discover you've missed a pivotal subskill or body of enabling knowledge, then adjusting your instruction to include the omitted building block is clearly in order.

• *Did I sequence my learning progression's building blocks optimally?* If you've been teaching your students using a learning progression whose building blocks are out of order, then re-do the order of those building blocks and see if a re-teach using the revised sequence does the trick.

• *Was my explanation of the content or skill being sought sufficiently clear?* Most of us think that we do a pretty decent job of explaining things to others. But, of course, we often don't. See if you can retrace the essential elements of any important explanations to your students to discern if there were shortcomings in those explanations. A new and improved explanation might just be what's needed.

• *Do I need to model what my students are supposed to achieve?* Many students have trouble grasping how to proceed until they have seen a teacher, or another student, provide an example of the kinds of intellectual behavior being sought. Thus, if your previous instruction contained no modeling, or insufficient modeling, then the addition of such modeling might be just what your instructional sequence needs.

• *Have my students been on the receiving end of sufficient guided or independent practice opportunities?* As I indicated, this was my personal instructional fault in almost all of my less-than-acceptable instructional efforts. If you have given what you regard as sufficient practice opportunities to your students, I'll bet you haven't. (I suspect I'm biased on this one.) Additional doses of guided and independent practice almost always saved my weak instructional designs. They might save yours.

• *Have I consulted colleagues to get their ideas about how to adjust a set of so-so instructional activities?* All of us get in ruts from time to time. When trying to figure out what to adjust, we just come up dry. At moments like this, it is often helpful to enlist "fresh eyes" to look at an instructional sequence and offer ideas about how to make it work better. You are not under any obligation to implement suggestions snared from colleagues, and you can certainly deep-six those ideas you regard as patently silly. However, given a few dozen oysters, one sometimes finds a pearl or two.

These few illustrative questions certainly do not exhaust the things you might consider when trying to answer the what-to-adjust question. In truth, most teachers who are serious about implementing the formative assessment process will, in time, come up with a collection of questions such as these that can provide potential cues about what might be adjusted when trying to improve an instructional sequence. The more systematic a teacher can be about such adjustments, the better it will be for the teacher's students.

Students' En Route Information Needs

Instructional monitoring can pay off for students as much as it can for teachers. Where students are concerned, the focus is on the monitoring of *learning tactics*—that is, the way in which students are attempting to learn whatever it is they're attempting to learn. And just as formative assessment can supply evidence to help teachers decide if they should alter their instructional procedures, formative assessment can supply evidence to help students decide if they should alter the way they're trying to learn. The intended consequence of supplying en route information to both teachers and students is identical: improved student learning.

As we've just discussed, the two key instructional decisions for teachers are whether to adjust instruction and, if adjustment is warranted, what aspects of instruction to adjust. It's pretty much the same for students. If, during any part of an ongoing instructional sequence, students are supplied with assessment-based information about how well they're learning, then those students need to decide *whether* they need to make any changes in how they're trying to learn something. If the need for change is indicated, students then need decide *what* that change in their learning tactics should be.

Two Preliminary Considerations

Before getting into *when* and *how* issues related to student-focused formative assessment, there are two preliminary considerations to address: (1) optimal feedback mechanisms and (2) the grading of students' performances within the formative assessment process. If you are an experienced educator, you've most likely already given some thought to each of these topics. But in case you haven't, let's take this pair of instructionally relevant issues out for a quick spin.

Feedback. Providing students with feedback is not the same thing as formative assessment. However, the formative assessment process, when it focuses on helping students, certainly includes providing those students with appropriate feedback. In a comprehensive, practitioner-oriented research review on feedback's contribution to the improvement of student learning, Valerie J. Shute (2007) offers a definition that nicely captures the essential mission of what she refers to as *formative feedback*: "Formative feedback represents information communicated to the learner that is intended to modify her thinking or behavior for the purpose of improving learning" (p. 4).

But what sorts of feedback are optimal for enhancing students' learning? Empirical investigations have shed ample light on this issue. Teachers might give students very general information about the quality of performances, communicated in the form of an overall grade of A to F or in a percent of points earned, such as "78 out of 100." That's one extreme, and it's clearly at the *general* end of any sort of feedback continuum. In contrast, teachers could supply their students with very detailed feedback on their performance by offering suggestions on what students should work on to improve, or by writing copious comments on essays or in shared journals. Teachers could even supply actual activities that students might undertake in an effort to enhance learning.

The overriding purpose of providing students with good feedback is that it helps them identify where they currently are in relation to where they are going (the curricular aim being sought). In addition, good feedback also helps students see what they must do in order to master a given curricular aim. Fortunately, most researchers who delve into feedback are in pretty solid agreement about what makes feedback good. Let's look, then, at four attributes of effective feedback.

Effective feedback is skill focused. Teachers must be sure their feedback clarifies what each individual student must do in order to proceed toward mastery of the curricular aims being sought. The point is never to compare the performance of one student with the performance of any other student. In fact, research suggests that kind of *normative feedback* can often make a student's performance worse (Kluger & Denisi, 1996). Care must be taken so the feedback to students is linked to the cognitive skill being assessed rather than the specific task intended to determine students' skill mastery.

Effective feedback is directive. It provides students with one or more directions about what they might do to narrow the gap between where they currently are and where they need to be. Wiliam and Thompson (2008) contend that "to be formative, feedback needs to contain an implicit or explicit recipe for future action" (p. 61). In a perfect educational world, a teacher would not just provide feedback containing suggestions as to what sorts of things students might do to improve but would actually supply explicit, "here's-how-to-get-better" instructional activities. In our real world, teachers must be realistic about how elaborate their feedback to students can be, but the more instructionally directive feedback is, the more likely it is to be effective. Teachers shouldn't worry about diagnosing the perfect learning solution: the one-and-only learning tactic adjustment each student must make in order to improve; it's enough to offer each student alternatives—well-reasoned *suggestions* about what might be done.

Effective feedback is timely. Students need to receive feedback early enough in the learning process so that they have time to adjust their learning tactics before it's instructionally too late. To illustrate, if a teacher were carrying out a 10-day unit focused on students' mastery of a particular subskill, and students received feedback from several en route assessments on Day 9, it's unlikely they would have time to realistically act on that feedback before the unit's conclusion. Even the most adroit adjustments in students' learning tactics won't work if these adjustments aren't allowed time to work.

Effective feedback is simple. It is often said that a little knowledge can be dangerous. Well, too much knowledge can be equally hazardous—especially to teachers. Because teachers will almost always know far more than their students about the content being considered in class, there's a constant danger that the teacher's feedback will be too sophisticated for the students to make sense of. A tension exists, of course, between supplying feedback that's sufficiently elaborated versus supplying feedback that's *too* elaborated. Clearly, what's called for in this instance is another invocation of the "Goldilocks Rule," wherein teachers frame the complexity level of their feedback to students so that it's "just right." What teachers always need to keep reminding themselves is that the feedback they are supplying to their students is supposed to stimulate *action* on the part of the student. Thus, teachers must take care not to overwhelm students with too much information focused on too many weaknesses, lest students conclude that they're hopeless cases and simply give up. Better to identify the most important of a student's weaknesses—improvable weaknesses, that is—and make those the focus of improvement-oriented feedback.

It's also really important to point the student in a sensible improvement direction. If descriptive feedback is supposed to let Maddie know what to do in order to move effectively toward mastery of a sought-for curricular aim, then Maddie must understand how to go about reducing the gap between where she is and where she wants to be. Teachers should use kid-friendly language and spell out what needs to be done.

All feedback, of course, need not be centered on students' shortcomings. There are many opportunities for teachers to laud things that students do well. I can recall, as a second-year teacher, seeing one of the students in my speech class begin to employ really effective gestures for the very first time as he presented his in-class speeches. (Previously, his gestures had been so exaggerated and artificial that he resembled a robot on weak batteries.) At the end of the first speech in which he employed really natural gestures, I definitely let him know to keep it up or, in his case, to keep it toned down.

The grading issue. If the prominent function of formative assessment is to help students learn more effectively and more efficiently, then teachers will need to engage in serious rethinking of the role classroom tests play in determining students' grades. It's true that testing is part of a worldwide, time-honored tradition of comparing students with one another (those whose performance hits this mark earn As; those whose performances fall below this mark earn Fs), but it is fundamentally wrongheaded to try to use a test to help students monitor their own learning while, at the same time, using the results of that test to grade or rank those students. It's also true that teachers in most settings *must* give grades, and that tests—some tests—will likely play a part in grade determination. But the vast majority of classroom tests, the ones intended to help students better manage their own learning, *should not be graded*.

Why? Because it is imperative not to contaminate the learning dividends derived from classroom formative assessments by needlessly affixing grades to students' performances on those assessments. Why, you might ask, does grade giving contaminate the learning dividends? The answer is that formative assessment's focus is on getting students to *learn*, not outperform other students. Teachers who make most tests nongraded can help students realize that the function of tests is to "help me learn," not determine who is "smarter" than who. When tests aren't graded, mistakes morph from something "bad" to something helpful—because mistakes can be corrected. What's crucial is not along-the-way errors but the skills and knowledge kids end up with when instruction is finished.

Making formative assessments a pivotal part of the classroom instructional process will not take place overnight. It will take teachers *and* students a good long while to accept the idea most classroom tests can function in a way intended to improve learning, not evaluate students. Teachers will obviously need to let students know, well in advance, which tests are intended for grade determination ("Because of the district's need for me to supply grades, the upcoming classroom test on Wednesday will be used for grading purposes"). But such tests really should be as few as teachers can get away with.

When to Supply Students with Assessment Information

As we've noted, when it comes to formative assessment, more formal testing is not automatically the best bet. It's important for teachers to weigh the time demands of administering en route tests and quizzes against the teaching and learning benefits such assessment evidence can help bring about. The teacher's aim here is to give students information they need to improve their own learning, and, frankly, students are likely to pay more attention to the results of a modest number of formative tests than to a ceaseless torrent of test results. It is possible to overwhelm almost anyone with too much evidence. Kids are equally overwhelmable, and kids who are struggling in school can be particularly so.

It's up to each teacher using formative assessment to decide the number of evidence-gathering (and, thus, information-supplying) occasions that is optimal for every particular instructional situation. Again, the best framework to follow is the learning progression for the curricular aim being pursued. Because students will need to master all the building blocks present in that progression, students need to receive assessment-elicited evidence regarding their status with respect to each subskill and body of enabling knowledge included in the progression.

Teachers must, therefore, plan to incorporate *at least one* formative assessment opportunity for each of the subskills or bodies of enabling knowledge identified in a target curricular aim's learning progression. I also recommend they employ a dress rehearsal assessment directly measuring students' mastery of the most significant curricular aims they're pursuing at a point that there's still time for an instructional adjustment (on the teacher's part) and a learning tactic adjustment (on the student's part).

When deciding when to gather formative assessment evidence, it's less important that teachers "get it totally right" than it is for them to devote some serious thinking to this issue. Teachers are professionals, and professionals possess expertise. In this instance, teachers need to bring a pile of their pedagogical expertise to bear on the question of how often—and when—to formatively assess their students.

How to Gather Evidence for Students' Use

With one exception, the kinds of formative assessment procedures teachers might want to use for their own purposes are usually suitable to provide students with their own adjustment-related evidence. Because student-signaled status reports such as the traffic signal technique represent only students' judgments and contain little objective assessment-based evidence, such approaches don't provide students the kind of information they need to make evidence-based decisions. Other than student-signaled status systems, however, the typical sorts of selected-response and constructed-response assessments can prove quite useful for supplying students with a picture of how well they're currently performing in relation to where they should be performing.

Feedback's role in guiding learning tactic adjustments. As noted, to the extent possible, feedback to students within the formative assessment process should provide guidance on how students might improve their learning. Teachers should supply students not only with a score report for every test used for formative purposes but also with ideas about what that student might do to improve the level of understanding the score report represents. These could be activities such as suitable readings, on-target practice exercises, or even teaming up with a capable classmate for a session of peer tutoring.

The relevance of rubrics. Rubrics, typically employed to help evaluate constructed-response or performance assessments such as essay tests, speeches, and projects, can supply students with helpful guidance. Because the skill-specific evaluative criteria set out in a well-conceived rubric can supply students with a judgmental framework for self-appraisal, such rubrics are extraordinarily important in a formative assessment context.

To help students appraise their own work, teachers should be sure everyone in the class is familiar with each rubric's key evaluative features. It is often helpful, incidentally, to start out this process by having students use a rubric to evaluate each other's work via peer assessment. (Interestingly, many students can more readily become conversant with a rubric's evaluative criteria when asked to apply those criteria in judging a classmate's performance rather than in judging their own performances.) After students have become comfortable using a rubric in a peer assessment context, they are ready to move on to rubric-guided self-assessment.

Teachers will find that the frequent inclusion of peer assessments and self-assessments in the formative assessment process turns out to be a prominent determiner of how well a teacher's formative assessment strategies are likely to work. The more peer assessing and self-assessing that goes on, the more successful formative assessment is likely to be. The reason for this increased success is that when students are really taking a meaningful part in their side of the formative assessment equation through peer and self-assessment, they tend to internalize the rubrics required to conduct such assessments. Truly internalized rubrics can have a powerful impact on the way a student approaches problems to which those rubrics are relevant.

Formative Assessment in Four Flavors

In this chapter's look at the monitoring of instruction and learning, the third in my recommended four-step approach to a teacher's instructional decision making, you have seen that essentially all of a teacher's monitoring activities are consistent with the use of formative assessment. Formative assessment, therefore, provides a sensible organizing framework for a teacher's monitoring of instruction and learning.

Elsewhere (Popham, 2008), I have suggested that there is clarity-enhancing merit in viewing formative assessment not as a unitary entity but, rather, as four distinguishable levels:

- *Level 1: Teachers' Instructional Adjustments.* In this first level of formative assessment, teachers collect assessment-elicited evidence about students in order to decide whether to modify current or immediately upcoming instruction.
- *Level 2: Students' Learning Tactic Adjustments.* The second level of formative assessment involves supplying students with assessment-elicited evidence so those students can, *all by themselves*, decide if they wish to alter how they are currently trying to learn what they are supposed to be learning.
- *Level 3: Classroom Climate Shift.* This third level of formative assessment requires a comprehensive change in the atmosphere of a class so that a traditional climate can be replaced with one in which the teacher and students collaboratively use ongoing assessment-based evidence to promote improved learning.
- *Level 4: Schoolwide Implementation.* The fourth level of formative assessment focuses on getting it used more widely in school, in districts, regionally, and nationally.

Clearly, there are meaningful relationships among these four levels of formative assessment, but there are also significant differences. For example, Level 1 formative assessment (teachers' instructional adjustments) can be implemented by teachers without installing any of the other three levels. Similarly, it's possible for a teacher to install Level 2 formative assessment (students' learning tactic adjustments) without also implementing Level 1. For Level 3 formative assessment (classroom climate shift), however, it is imperative for *both* Levels 1 and 2 to be in place, as the comprehensive change in the atmosphere of a classroom foreseen in Level 3 requires that both a teacher and the teacher's students routinely use assessment evidence to make warranted adjustments in what they are doing. Finally, Level 4 formative assessment (schoolwide implementation) calls for the expanded use of one or more of the other three levels of formative assessment.

Distinguishing among different levels of formative assessment will make this important process easier to understand and, therefore, easier to explain to others. If we accept formative assessment as the framework for teachers to monitor the ongoing quality of their instructional efforts, we must also agree that teachers need to understand both its essential features and its nuances.

 Chapter Check-Back

- The mission of instructional monitoring is to help teachers decide whether to make adjustments in their instructional activities and to help students decide whether to make adjustments in their learning tactics.
- The process of formative assessment provides both teachers and students with the information they need to determine if instructional or learning tactic adjustments are needed as well as the kinds of adjustments these should be.
- Teachers' choices regarding when to collect formative assessment evidence and how to collect it are best informed by the learning progressions underlying significant curricular aims.
- Some of the many specific measurement techniques teachers may employ to collect en route formative assessment evidence have the additional benefit of promoting students' engagement in the lesson.

- Feedback to students is most effective when it is task focused, directive, timely, and simple; it is least effective when it comes in the form of grades.
- Formative assessment can be divided into four levels: teachers' instructional adjustments, students' learning tactic adjustments, a classroom climate shift, and schoolwide implantation; use of Level 1 formative assessment is a commendable goal for most teachers.

Suggestions for Further Reading

Leahy, S., Lyon, C., Thompson, M., & Wiliam, D. (2005, November). Classroom asssessment: Minute by minute, day by day. *Educational Leadership, 63*(3), 18–24.

Leahy and her colleagues set forth a set of five powerful strategies for relying on the process of formative assessment to enhance students' learning. This Educational Leadership *article is required reading for any teacher who sincerely wishes to monitor students' progress and make assessment-dictated adjustments in the instruction itself and in the way students are trying to learn.*

McMillan, J. H. (Ed.). (2007). *Formative classroom assessment: Theory into practice.* New York: Teachers College Press.

This collection of essays by leading authorities in the field of educational assessment provides readers with some excellent insights regarding our currently evolving understandings of what's involved in the real-world applications of formative assessment.

Stiggins, R. (2006, November/December). Assessment *for* learning: A key to motivation and achievement. *Edge, 2.*

In this 20-page booklet distributed by Phi Delta Kappa, Stiggins argues that the skillful use of classroom assessment for *learning (rather than assessment* of *learning) can make an enormous contribution to students' motivation, confidence, and achievement. Stiggins contends that real progress flowing from classroom assessment is unlikely unless (1) the framework of achievement expectations is reflected in all exercises and scoring schemes for assessment, (2) standards-based schools are in place, and (3) the assessments used are accurate. Indicators of sound classroom assessment practice conclude this easily read booklet.*

6

Evaluating Instruction

Let's assume you're a teacher who has played the instructional game with consummate care. You've carefully selected a collection of crackerjack curricular aims for your students, perhaps prioritizing from the set of officially mandated aims. You've designed what you believed to be a scintillating and well-sequenced set of instructional activities to promote students' attainment of those aims. And you've employed formative assessment to monitor your ongoing instructional activities. Based on such along-the-way evidence, you've made several key adjustments in your instruction, and you've even used the same formative assessment evidence to prompt your students to adjust their learning tactics. Yes, based on this sort of Assumption Land scenario, you seem to have carried out instruction in precisely the way you should have. But here's the crunch-time question about your instruction: *Did it work?*

For teachers, coming up with an accurate answer means returning to the kind of ends-means thinking introduced back in Chapter 1. You'll recall that when teachers initially choose a set of curricular aims for their students, they're actually laying out the *intended* ends their instruction is supposed to accomplish: the knowledge, skills, and affect they hope their students will attain as a consequence of having been taught.

Thereafter, when teachers plan, implement, and monitor their instruction, all those instructional activities deal with the *means* part of the ends-means model.

How can teachers tell if their instructional means were effective? As you've already guessed, to answer this question, teachers need to focus on what their students have learned. Did students actually attain the desired ends—the knowledge, skills, and affect represented by the curricular aims being pursued? Only by focusing on ends-attainment can teachers discover whether their means actually succeeded.

Experienced teachers typically *want* to evaluate their own instruction because, as professionals, they want to do a good job. They know that the better a teacher's instruction is, the better students' learning will be. But the accountability movement also means that an increasing number of educational policymakers are now calling for rigorous, externally imposed evaluation of teachers. And school districts are complying. Accordingly, as you proceed through this chapter, you may find it useful to distinguish between *volitional instructional evaluation by the teacher* and *mandatory instructional evaluation by others*. When teachers are obliged to carry out a "for others" appraisal of their own instruction, there are several key alterations called for in how a teacher tackles such an appraisal task. In general, those alterations revolve around how to enhance the *credibility* of evidence bearing on the quality of a teacher's instruction.

Evidence of Instructional Effectiveness

Relying once more on an ends-means paradigm, we see the most important evidence of instruction's effectiveness flows from the degree to which students learned what they were supposed to learn. When teachers are obliged to supply external authorities with evidence related to curricular-aim attainment, it makes sense to collect evidence related to the most significant curricular aims. Realistically, most external authorities are apt to be more impressed by students' achievement of a modest number of very demanding, high-level cognitive skills than by students' mastery of a more numerous collection of less demanding curricular aims.

In Chapter 5, we were looking at *formative* evidence of students' achievement to use in instructional improvement. In this chapter, however, we are focusing on *summative* evidence of a teacher's success. Generally, when it comes to summative evidence of instructional effectiveness, there are three main types to consider: *product evidence, process evidence,* and *affective evidence.*

Product Evidence

Proof of students' curricular-aim attainment is best obtained through classroom assessment and well-aligned, properly timed, and instructionally sensitive external achievement tests.

Results of teacher-developed classroom assessments. Ideally, most assessments to be used in measuring students' mastery of curricular aims will already have been developed—or at least will already have been conceptualized—as part of the teacher's early-on efforts to clarify curricular aims (see Chapter 4). If such is not the case, then a teacher will definitely need to create one or more assessment devices to determine whether students have actually attained the intended outcomes embodied in the teacher's curricular aims. I recommend any of the numerous assessment tactics described in Chapter 2. Whether teachers rely on traditional selected-response items and constructed-response items or on more innovative assessment approaches, such as portfolio assessment or performance tests, the guiding question is always the same: *What assessment-based evidence will allow me to reach a valid inference about my students' curricular-aim status?*

Scores on the right kinds of external achievement tests. Teachers may be able to employ students' performances on external achievement tests to evaluate the effectiveness of their instruction, provided that (1) what's measured by an annual accountability test meshes satisfactorily with a teacher's own curricular aims, (2) the test is administered at a point in the school year so that the teacher receives results in time to determine the success of recently completed instructional activities, and (3) the test is instructionally sensitive, as described in Chapter 2. If any of these conditions is not met, the evidence yielded by external achievement tests will be essentially meaningless for judging a teacher's instructional effectiveness.

Of course, teachers may find themselves in a setting where the results of external accountability tests not meeting these conditions *do* play a role in determining the quality of a teacher's instruction. All I can do is urge teachers and administrators to not attach *genuine* evaluative significance to students' scores on such exams . . . and to investigate some of the recommendations I will provide in Chapter 7.

Process Evidence

Teachers can't accurately judge their own instructional effectiveness by relying only on personal perceptions of "how well the instruction went." Similarly, the personal judgment of outside observers—even highly trained, super-sophisticated observers who spend scads of time watching a teacher teach—is almost certain to be irrelevant. For all its long tradition, classroom observation, with or without guiding rubrics that highlight research-based effective processes, really is more a tradition than it is an accurate, standalone means of measuring teaching effectiveness.

Because of teaching's inordinate complexity, based on a particular teacher teaching particular kids particular content in a particular setting on a particular day, there's simply no *process* evidence of instructional quality (what teachers or students do) that can ever override *product* evidence of instructional effectiveness (the ends they attain). Process evidence focuses on means; an evaluator's concern must be ends.

One exception to the can't-tell-by-looking rule occurs when observers of a teacher's classroom procedures discover a teacher is engaged in classroom conduct that any sensible person would regard as super-shoddy. For instance, let's say you spent a few class periods observing a colleague whose classroom management skills are decidedly underdeveloped. Not only were most students engaged in noisy personal conversations, but the teacher simply read aloud a series of textbook sections previously assigned as homework. Whether or not any students actually *heard* this reading, you could not determine. Now, given such a hypothetically disastrous set of classroom activities, you could probably conclude, with a fair degree of accuracy, that the teacher's instruction was ineffective.

But it doesn't always work the other way. Suppose you were observing another colleague's instruction, and what you saw looked flat-out fabulous. The teacher did all the sensible instructional things set forth in Chapter 4. She clarified her curricular expectations for students, provided ample time-on-task activities for those students, and relied frequently on formative assessment to adjust her ongoing instruction. You, as a classroom observer, would most likely conclude that the teacher's instruction was stellar. You'd *probably* be right. But you might not be.

Even those teachers whose classroom activities seem wonderful to observers can flop instructionally. The instructional procedures that seem so laudable might somehow rub those particular students (because of the students' previous educational experiences) the wrong way. Although odds are that theoretically praiseworthy instructional procedures will truly warrant praise, the proof of the quality of any instructional process must be in the "kid consequences" it causes. And that's why even high-quality process observations of what transpires in classrooms will never—except in the case of staggeringly rotten teaching procedures—prove as evaluatively persuasive as will evidence bearing on students' assessed attainment of curricular ends.

Affective Aim Evidence

For teachers setting out to gauge the effectiveness of their own instruction, evidence of worthwhile shifts in students' attitudes, interests, and values can be every bit as important as students' cognitive accomplishments. Let's face it: If a middle school math teacher gets students to learn lots of nifty numerical notions but, in doing so, also gets them to detest mathematics, then those negative affective consequences might completely cancel out any of the students' cognitive math attainments. Ideally, teachers will routinely adopt at least a few affective curricular aims so that students will be, at minimum, as positively disposed toward the subjects being taught when instruction is over as they were when instruction began.

Documented affective changes—outcomes such as an increase in students' "eagerness to learn new things"—can be powerful data to persuade outside evaluators that what went on in class is having a potent and positive effect. External teacher evaluators are rarely given evidence of a teacher's role relative to students' attitudes, interests, or values, and the atypical nature of such affective evidence can have an attention-arresting impact.

Wild Card Evidence: Unintended Consequences of Instruction

A teacher's intended outcomes for students should play the prominent role in gauging a teacher's effectiveness. Did the teacher's instructional design achieve the intended consequences? Did the students master target curricular aims? Did they acquire the skills, knowledge, and affective characteristics the teacher set out for them? However, not all of what happens to students is *intended*. We must care about the total array of what happens to students irrespective of whether what happened was planned or not. And this is why teachers must always be attentive to the possibilities that important *unintended consequences* of instruction may have taken place. Such unforeseen consequences (both positive and negative) can, and should, alter judgments about a teacher's instructional success.

To illustrate, suppose Mr. Cunningham, a high school mathematics teacher, is teaching in a district where his students must pass an introductory algebra course in order to graduate. Let's say that by the end of the school year, he has collected ample evidence that almost all of his 30 students have displayed mastery of the course's 5 major algebra objectives. That sounds pretty good. But suppose it turns out that there were 36 students enrolled in his algebra class at the beginning of the school year. From September to June, six students were performing so poorly that they despaired of passing the test, concluded they'd never graduate, and dropped out of school to spare themselves what seemed like an awful lot of futile effort. To put it another way, fully 20 percent of Mr. Cunningham's Algebra I students left school because of what went on in his class. This unintended, clearly negative consequence really ought to factor into that teacher's judgment of his instructional success, and it ought to prompt him to rethink what he is doing instructionally.

Unintended consequences can also be positive. For example, suppose Ms. Chen has been assigned to teach a middle school English course in which all of the enrolled students are reading well below grade level. She sets out to deal with a number of language arts curricular aims in the course, but her overall push is toward getting students to become more capable readers. As she spends time helping her students to master the basics of reading, employing such approaches as phonics and the use of context clues to determine words' meaning, she also inaugurates a peer-reading strategy in which pairs of students read aloud to one another. Ms. Chen works to make this pair reading a positive experience by selecting materials tailored to students' reading levels. As the school year goes by, she sees progress in terms of her students' overall reading skills but is still surprised to hear from the school librarian that many of the peer-pair students are checking out books to read on their own, sometimes in pairs and sometimes solo. In short, it appears that Ms. Chen's approach is fostering not only improved reading skills (as must be demonstrated by more conventional assessments) but also decisively more positive affect toward reading itself. Students who, heretofore, were apathetic or intimidated by reading are now choosing to read unassigned materials. That sort of unanticipated effect is surely positive and should certainly be included in Ms. Chen's appraisal of her instructional success.

My chief point here is that when teachers evaluate their own instruction, they should attend first to whether their students have attained the curricular aims set out for them. But they must also be on the lookout for any sort of unintended consequences of their instruction, either positive or negative. Sometimes, at the end of a significant chunk of instruction, administering an open-ended anonymous questionnaire to students might help a teacher pick up insights regarding unforeseen effects of instruction.

How to Collect Evaluative Evidence

If the bulk of evidence to evaluate a teacher's instructional effectiveness is going to come from assessments revealing how well students have reached that teacher's curricular aims, the question remains of when and how a teacher should corral this sort of summative assessment-based evidence. Let's turn now to three possible evidence-gathering designs teachers might wish to employ in evaluating their own instruction.

The Post-Test-Only Design

One of the most elementary data-gathering designs that comes to mind when someone wants to evaluate a teacher's instruction is a simple after-instruction approach known as the *post-test-only design* and illustrated in Figure 6.1.

One look at the figure might tip you to a serious drawback of this approach. Because there's no assessment of students *prior* to instruction, it's impossible to isolate the impact of the teacher's instruction. Maybe the reason Mr. Evans's 5th graders aced his carefully crafted assessment aimed at measuring their mastery of an inquiry-based approach to science is not because the 10 weeks of instructional attention he devoted to the topic was so stellar but because his current crop of 5th graders were all in Ms. Miles's 4th grade class, where she built her *entire* instructional strategy around a science-as-inquiry model.

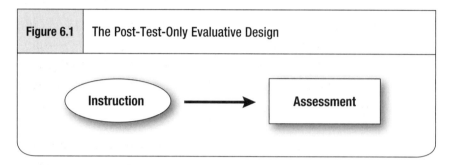

| Figure 6.1 | The Post-Test-Only Evaluative Design |

The fatal shortcoming of a post-test-only design is that Mr. Evans (or anyone else who uses it) can't tell whether students' post-instruction performances are chiefly attributable to a teacher's instruction or reflect what students had learned prior to that instruction. Some teachers and administrators actually place a great deal of confidence in this evidence-gathering approach, perhaps because we all tend to see what we want to see in these sorts of evaluative situations. If a colleague of yours truly fails to recognize how the absence of evidence prior to instruction diminishes the usefulness of this data-gathering design, be gentle. And then encourage that colleague to try something better.

The Pre-Test/Post-Test Design

To address the obvious weakness of the post-test-only design, many teachers prefer to employ the *pre-test/post-test design*, which is illustrated in Figure 6.2. As you can see, in this data-gathering model, assessment occurs both prior to and following instruction. Discerning the impact of instruction is a matter of comparing students' pre-test performances with their post-test performances. The resulting difference can be attributed chiefly to the effects of the teacher's instruction.

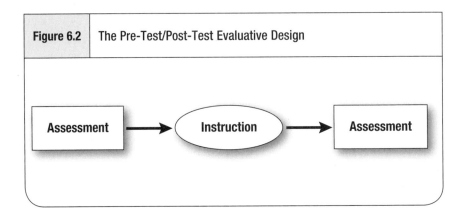

Figure 6.2 | The Pre-Test/Post-Test Evaluative Design

Assessment → Instruction → Assessment

As you may realize, there's a loophole in the logic that must be employed with this particular data-gathering design. That difficulty stems from the unarguable reality that kids grow. As they grow, it's likely their skills and knowledge will naturally develop—even without one minute of formal instruction—notably in areas such as communication skills, psychomotor skills, and the ability to reason. Accordingly, I urge teachers using this design to evaluate their own instructional effectiveness to greet improvements in post-test performances with measured enthusiasm rather than flat-out jubilation. This caution is especially applicable when teachers compare pre-test data gathered at the beginning of a school year with post-test data gathered at the school year's end.

There's another serious problem with the pre-test/post-test design, and it's known as *pre-test reactivity*. Because students' reactions to the pre-test may alter how those students react to the instruction itself, there's a real possibility that such pre-test-influenced reactions will make it difficult to tell how much of students' post-test performances are attributable to the teacher's instruction versus how much of those post-test performances were simply *pre-test stimulated*.

To illustrate, suppose a middle school biology teacher began a semester's worth of instruction by giving her students, as a pre-assessment, the same 10-item test she plans to use as an end-of-semester exam. Suppose further that the biology test contained two very memorable constructed-response items requiring students to (1) describe in detail how to identify an unnamed "mystery leaf" specimen and (2) indicate the positive and negative consequences of how marsupials pouch-protect their young offspring.

Thanks to the attention-grabbing power of both pre-test items, during the semester many students in the class paid special attention to both in-class and out-of-class information related to leaf identifying and marsupial pouching. Thus, when the end-of-semester 10-item exam was administered, there was a substantial improvement in students' test scores. Was this improvement a factor of the teacher's excellent overall instruction, or was it a function of pre-test reactivity, related to students' stellar performances on the pair of memorable pre-test items? It's really tough to tell.

The intuitive way around the problem of pre-test reactivity is to create equally difficult test forms—ones that contain different items but measure students' skills and knowledge in essentially the same way. This approach *would* work *if* truly equidifficult test forms could be easily constructed. Unfortunately, they can't. It is genuinely difficult and remarkably time-consuming for teachers to generate two test forms that, with no difference in difficulty, assess students' mastery of the same curricular aims. This is something I learned firsthand. Earlier in my career, I headed a test development group that created high-stakes accountability tests for about a dozen states. One of those states was Texas. For the Texas test's writing items, we were supposed to supply three writing prompts that would present the same degree of challenge to all students. Well, our staff produced 20 prompts that we thought were equally difficult. Then we tried them out with large samples of Texas students: 1,000 students per prompt. There were 20,000 students involved in the tryout, each of them writing an essay on one of the hopefully equidifficult new prompts as well as an essay on an "anchor prompt" that all students completed. By comparing students' performances on the anchor prompt and the other prompt that they had received, we could tell how difficult each of the 20 new prompts was in relation to each other. Well, when we looked at the final data, only 4 of the 20 new prompts turned out to be genuinely equidifficult.

If a pre-test and post-test differ appreciably in difficulty, as they almost always will, the potential for evaluative misinterpretations abounds. If students' pre-test-to-post-test scores improve simply because the post-test was easier, the test-based inference (that the students have mastered the material and that the teacher's instruction was wonderful) is invalid. The teacher won't know that his instruction went astray or that students didn't learn as well as he'd hoped they would. Although his instruction could use modification, it won't get it. Likewise, if a too tough post-test leads to lower post-test scores, the inference that the teacher's instruction was weak is equally invalid. Not only might this lead him to modify instruction that's working perfectly well, but this evidence of "ineffectiveness," if required by outside evaluators, might lead to serious consequences.

Despite its shortcomings, the pre-test/post-test evaluative design has much to commend it. As long as teachers can be attentive to the potential misinterpretations arising from students' natural growth and pre-test reactivity, this before-and-after design can supply useful evidence regarding whether a teacher's instruction is working well.

Back in Chapter 3, I mentioned that teachers might occasionally wish to employ *item sampling*, an approach in which each student is directed to complete only some of a test's items. As noted, item-sampling works remarkably well as a *pre-test* in the pre-test/post-test design because item sampling can supply teachers with a reasonably accurate estimate of students' entry-level achievement, but item sampling markedly minimizes the effect of pre-test reactivity. This occurs because students get mostly different post-test items (on their "complete" post-test) than the pre-test items they received (on their "partial" pre-test).

I'll introduce several techniques for strengthening the basic pre-test/post-test design during our consideration of the final data-gathering design that teachers can use when evaluating their instructional effectiveness. Let's turn to it now.

The Split-and-Switch Design

If a teacher has a reasonably large class of 30 or so students, there's a modification of the pre-test/post-test design that can be useful for evaluating the teacher's instructional success. It's called the *split-and-switch design,* and I want to show you how it works. Because the procedural details of the split-and-switch design can be confusing, the easiest way for me to explain it involves your assuming that you are the teacher who is using this data-gathering design.

1. *Create two test forms.* To get underway, you'll need two forms of the test you're going to use as a pre-test and as a post-test. The two forms ought to be *similar* in degree of difficulty but need not be completely equivalent in difficulty. We can refer to the two forms as *Test Form 1* and *Test Form 2.* The two forms of the test can consist of selected-response items, constructed-response items, or a combination of both.

2. *Split the class.* Next, randomly split your class into two roughly equal *half-class* groups, perhaps by counting halfway down your class roster so that all students whose last names start with the letters *A* through *L* are in *Half-Class A*, while all students whose last names start with the letters *M* through *Z* are in *Half-Class B*.

3. *Pre-assess, using a different test form for each half class.* Administer a different test form to each half-class, asking students to write only their names—on the back of their completed test—and explicitly asking them *not* to write the date.

4. *Collect and code the pre-tests.* If either of the two forms contains constructed-response items, you should then write an identifying code number on the back of the last page of students' completed tests so that you will be able to identify them as pre-tests at a later date. You might, for instance, use a three-number code, and make sure the middle number is always an even number. Any three-number code whose middle number is 0, 2, 4, 6, or 8, therefore, signifies that "this is a pre-test." (Note: At this point you can certainly look at students' pre-test responses for the purposes of planning your own instruction, but unless the tests contain *only* selected-response items, you should *not* write any scores on the actual test forms at this time.)

5. *Now, teach.* Teach up a storm! Instruct all your students to the very best of your ability for as long as you have allowed for the instruction:

perhaps a few weeks or perhaps an entire semester, if the curricular aim is sufficiently complex.

6. *Post-test, switching the test forms.* When instruction is complete, switch the test forms for post-testing. If Half-Class A took Test Form 1 as a pre-test, give that group Test Form 2 as a post-test. Similarly, if Half-Class B received Test Form 2 as a pre-test, give those students Test Form 1 as a post-test. Again, direct students to write their name of the back of their test but not the date.

7. *Collect and code the post-tests.* As before, assign code numbers to the post-tests so you can distinguish them, after consulting your codes, from the pre-tests. For instance, you could again use a three-number code, but this time, use an odd number in the middle to indicate the test was completed after instruction.

8. *Combine the pre-tests and the post-tests, then sort them by form.* Mix together all the copies of Test Form 1 (both the pre-tests and the post-tests), and do the same with the pre-tests and post-tests for Test Form 2.

9. *Score the tests, as blindly as possible.* If there is any substantial portion of your two test forms consisting of constructed-response items, at this point you should try to get *nonpartisan scorers* (colleagues or parents) to judge the quality of the mixed-together Test Form 1 responses and then the quality of mixed-together Test Form 2 responses. If your Test Forms are exclusively composed of selected-response items, there's really no need for nonpartisan scoring. You will be scoring your students' pre-tests and post-tests objectively because there are no evaluative judgments needed from you about students' constructed responses. All you need to do is make sure that you can tell which students' responses are pre-tests and which ones are post-tests.

10. *Re-sort into pre-test and post-tests, and compare the scores.* After all scoring has been done, consult the codes and sort the blind-scored papers into pre-tests and post-tests. Clearly, what you hope to see is a substantial improvement in students' post-test performances over their pre-test performances.

The split-and-switch design is illustrated in Figure 6.3. Notice that the appropriate comparisons, and there will be *two* such comparisons—the pre-test-to-post-test changes for Test Form 1 and the pre-test-to-post-test changes for Test Form 2— are signified by the broken arrows.

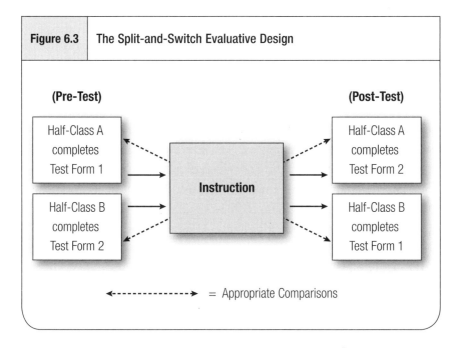

Figure 6.3 | **The Split-and-Switch Evaluative Design**

That this evaluative design provides *two* indications of whether your instruction promoted post-test improvement is one of its key strengths. Also, because the pre-test and post-test comparisons are made using the *very same test*, there will be no problems related to a difference in test form difficulty. Moreover, because your students have not previously seen, as a pre-test, the specific post-test items they will receive, the potentially confounding impact of pre-test reactivity is dramatically reduced.

Another strength of the split-and-switch design is that it works especially well for determining students' affective shifts. Affective pre-testing is particularly apt to sensitize students to what the teacher plans to emphasize during the pursuit of a curricular aim, making pre-test reactivity especially problematic.

Here's how you might use the split-and-switch design to gather evidence of instructional effectiveness relative to affective curricular aims.

Let's suppose you've opted to pursue four affective aims during a given school year: two dealing with students' *interest* in particular subject areas (for instance, science and social studies) and two dealing with students' *confidence* in being able to use key skills associated with two other subjects (for instance, reading and mathematics). What you might do is create two different affective inventories for your Test Form 1 and Test Form 2, each of which would consist of anonymously completed self-report devices similar to those described in Chapter 2. However, Test Form 1 would contain only items dealing with reading (confidence) and science (interest), and Test Form 2 would contain only items dealing with mathematics (confidence) and social studies (interest). Thus, a student who receives a Test Form 1 inventory prior to instruction would be getting a Test Form 2 inventory at the end of instruction. Recipients of Test Form 2 inventories prior to instruction would get a Test Form 1 inventory at instruction's close. Even though these affective inventories contain no constructed-response items (because total anonymity depends on selected-responses), the potential reactivity of the affective pre-assessments would be eliminated. At post-instruction time, all students would be responding for the first time to a new set of affective items, and the pre-to-post comparisons of your 50-percent samples would give you an accurate estimate of what's happening affectively in your entire class.

The split-and-switch design works well if you find yourself teaching reasonably large classes. But be warned that if you end up teaching classes of smaller than 20 students, the two half-classes used in the design will be so small that, even though they constitute a 50 percent sample of your full class, it's difficult to place much confidence in the degree to which those half-classes accurately represent the entire class. Anther caution to keep in mind when employing the split-and-switch design is the amount of administrative time it demands. There's a fair amount of hassle associated with using this data-gathering design, such as the creating of two forms, class splitting, test coding, test mixing, scoring, and comparing. Maximizing the credibility of any evaluation of your instructional success (as is particularly important when external authorities require such instructional evaluations) also involves rounding up nonpartisan judges to blind-score your students' mixed-together pre-tests and post-tests. And so it makes sense to employ a split-and-switch design for *only a few* of your most significant curricular aims—typically students' acquisition of very high-level cognitive skills.

And there's one more reason to use the split-and-switch approach only occasionally rather than every few weeks. Some of your students will begin to recognize what's going on with the switched test forms. They'll realize that if they received Test Form 2 as a pre-test, they'll be given Test Form 1 as a post-test and vice versa. Many students won't care all that much, one way or the other. But look for some of your most eager students to start asking a classmate who received "the other pre-test" what that pre-test covered. This trading of pre-test recollections, if widespread, tends to reduce the split-and-switch design's ability to suppress pre-test reactivity.

When to Use Which Design

We've now considered three different evaluative designs that can be used to assemble evidence regarding the success of a teacher's instruction. All three designs focus properly on what happens to students as a consequence of teaching. But all three designs, as you have seen, deal with students' post-instruction status in somewhat different ways. Here are some guidelines on when to use the various designs, based on the overall purpose of the instruction's evaluation.

For volitional instructional evaluation. For teachers trying to determine how well they've been teaching strictly for their own self-evaluative purposes, there is a role for all three of the data-gathering designs.

Teachers might choose to use the post-test-only design to give them a rough fix on how well they've taught some of the less significant of their curricular aims. They might also consider it for curricular aims they are fairly sure their students have not encountered before. If, for example, you're an elementary school teacher about to take your students into what your district curriculum guide assures you is their very first serious foray into world history, then it's likely much of those students' post-instruction knowledge of world history is going to be attributable to *your* instruction and not to someone else's. With novel content and brand new curricular aims, the post-test-only design can be a useful tool.

The pre-test/post-test design is well suited for evaluating instruction focused on the most important of a teacher's curricular goals, and teachers who can reduce the number of their curricular aims to a modest number will probably have the time *and energy* to use it. Item sampling provides a way to reduce the in-class time commitment required. If a teacher has sufficient confidence in the number of students responding to each item, then the insights the teacher can garner from item sampling are usually quite sound.

Finally, due to the administrative demands of the split-and-switch design, I recommend teachers employ it only to evaluate the success of instruction targeted at their most significant curricular aims and, beyond that, primarily when students' mastery of such aims is to be measured using some variation of constructed-response assessment procedures. Other than a reduction of pre-test reactivity, there's little additional payoff for a split-and-switch design when tests consist only of selected-response items.

External instructional evaluation. When the evaluation of teachers' instructional efforts is being *imposed* by others, a teacher's evaluative protocol should change considerably. In such instances it makes little sense to present the sort of evaluative evidence obtainable from a post-test-only approach. External authorities simply won't put any confidence in evidence that takes no account of students' pre-instruction entry status. And, as you have seen earlier, they usually shouldn't.

Teachers should assemble the bulk of the evaluative evidence using either the pre-test/post-test design or the split-and-switch design, using all the optional, credibility-enhancing bells and whistles available to them, including blind-scoring of mixed-together pre-tests and post-tests and patently nonpartisan scorers. When external teacher evaluation is afoot, it would be better to recruit a small group of parents or business people to serve as scorers than it would be for a teacher to enlist fellow teachers. Given appropriate training in the use of any required evaluative rubrics, these "citizen scorers" can do an excellent job while enhancing the impression of impartiality and, thus, bolstering the credibility of key evaluative data related to a teacher's instruction.

Teacher Evaluation: The Elusive Grail

The focus of this chapter has been on the evaluation of instruction. And such a focus splashes over into one of the most vexing problem areas of our field, namely, *teacher evaluation*. I'd like to consider that problem here, in this wrap-up section, but only briefly. Exercising an authorial prerogative, I'm going to toss out my own views on how to evaluate teachers. You may not agree with me, and that's fine. But I simply couldn't say farewell to a chapter focused on instructional evaluation without registering a few opinions regarding how teachers *ought* to be appraised.

My positions regarding teacher evaluation may not mesh with yours, but I'll bet mine have taken longer to develop. You see, as a research assistant in graduate school, my very first assignment dealt with teacher evaluation. My professor directed me to review all of the empirical investigations dealing with teacher evaluation published between 1900 and 1950. This took me months and months to do. And even though most of the studies I reviewed had been carried out many years earlier, the investigators who conducted those studies faced precisely the same set of difficulties that today's teacher evaluation researchers confront. Moreover, although many of those earlier researchers set out on a quest for a silver bullet that would permit the definitive appraisal of a teacher's competence, such a bullet was never found. It still hasn't been.

The insuperable obstacle to the creation of a sure-fire, cookie-cutter approach to teacher evaluation is *teaching's profound particularism*. A particular teacher, laden with a one-of-a-kind personal history and a distinctive genetic lineage, attempts to teach particular curricular aims to a particular set of students, each of whom brings an idiosyncratic background and a set of specific inherited aptitudes. This teaching goes on in a particular school directed by a particular school-site administrator, in a particular community. It is no overstatement to assert that each teacher functions in an instructional situation that is literally unique. Because evaluation typically involves comparison, evaluating a unique phenomenon isn't easy. For this reason, no system of teacher evaluation will be foolproof. Some stellar teachers will be regarded as not-so-stellar. Some tawdry teachers will be seen as acceptable. We'll never get a teacher evaluation system that's mistake-free, and those who toss out simplistic solutions, such as "determine a teacher's quality via students' scores on standardized tests," dramatically underestimate the nest of complexities known as teacher evaluation.

So, as someone who's been dipping in and out of the teacher evaluation research literature for more than 50 years, I've come to a conclusion about the only truly defensible way to evaluate a teacher's skill. Because of the inherent particularism enveloping a teacher's endeavors, I believe the evaluation of teaching must fundamentally rest on the *professional judgment of well-trained colleagues.*

Although it's been more than two decades since I first detailed this evaluative strategy (Popham, 1988), I continue to believe it outstrips every other evaluative approach introduced before or since. Its essential idea is that to evaluate a teacher sensibly, one must consider all sources of evidence that might bear on the teacher's quality. Such sources of evidence would include the following:

1. Students' performances on classroom tests
2. Students' affective status as measured by self-report inventories
3. Students' scores on standardized achievement tests
4. Administrators' ratings of a teacher's skill
5. Systematic observations of a teacher's classroom activities
6. Anonymous student ratings of their teachers
7. Teacher self-appraisals

Given the particulars surrounding a given teacher's instruction, some of these evidence sources will be more meaningful than will others. And that's where a panel of, say, three to five experienced teachers, intensively trained for this particular function, would enter the fray to judge the salience of any available evaluative evidence and then render an overall evaluation of a teachers' instructional competence relying on the most defensible evidence at hand.

Consider how such a panel might judge the evidence. Perhaps the teacher has collected a series of pre-test/post-test comparisons, blind-scored by parents using well-designed rubrics, and concluded that this evidence shows consistent growth in students' scores from before instruction to after instruction. The panel might give this finding considerable weight. Conversely, the panel might assign less weight to a principal's very positive rating if its members discover that the principal tends toward less-than-judiciousness and has consistently given every teacher in the school very high marks. The essence of this professional-judgment approach to teacher evaluation is that well-trained teachers (possibly even certified for this purpose) must weight the merits of as much relevant evidence as is available, then rely on the most persuasive evidence to form a synthesized judgment regarding a particular teacher's skill.

Will even a highly trained collection of colleagues occasionally err? Of course they will. But, given the essentially insurmountable problems of particularism surrounding the appraisal of a given teacher, a judgmentally rooted approach to teacher evaluation seems to be the most reasonable. Any approach to teacher appraisal that fails to address the uniqueness of a given teacher's situation is certain to be indefensible.

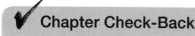 **Chapter Check-Back**

- The evaluation of a teacher's instructional success should be based on an ends-mean conception of teaching wherein the chief determinant of instructional quality is what students have learned.

- Evidence to consider in evaluating instructional success includes students' achievement of curricular aims documented in classroom tests; their scores on well-aligned, instructionally sensitive standardized achievement tests; and their responses on anonymous affective inventories.

- Unintended consequences of a teacher's instruction should factor into evaluative judgments of that teacher's instructional effectiveness.
- Evidence of instructional success may be collected through three evaluative designs, each with strengths and weaknesses: the post-test-only design, the pre-test/post-test design, and the split-and-switch design.
- When collecting evidence of instructional effectiveness, it is wise to distinguish between a teacher's volitional evaluative efforts and those evaluative requirements imposed by external authorities.
- A professional-judgment approach to teacher evaluation is the best and most defensible option.

Suggestions for Further Reading

Boudett, K. P., City, E. A., & Murnane, R. J. (Eds.) (2005). *Data wise: A step-by-step guide to using assessment results to improve teaching and learning.* Cambridge, MA: Harvard Education Press.

Although this book is focused on getting school leaders to understand how to use assessment results to evaluate the quality of instruction, its relevance to the interests of classroom teachers is considerable.

Stronge, J. H. (Ed.). (2006). *Evaluating teaching* (2nd ed.). Thousand Oaks, CA: Corwin Press.

Stronge has corralled a set of first-rate authors who set forth a series of practical recommendations regarding the design and implementation of a carefully conceived teacher evaluation system. Six of the book's 13 chapters focus on the assessment of teachers' performance.

7

Playing the New Game

Whenever the rules of the game are changed, the smartest players will adapt. In this concluding chapter, we'll be taking a more careful look at how instructional decision making is affected by the two assessment-based game-changers identified in Chapter 1, namely, (1) the documentation of the instructional dividends from formative classroom assessment and (2) the educational accountability movement, built on external accountability tests that purport to measure the effectiveness of instruction. And because I like to send readers off with concrete things to do, I'll be sharing several action options representing ways that you, as a teacher or administrator, might elevate your own instructional game or the instructional game of your colleagues.

The Advent of Classroom Formative Assessment

Most authorities agree that the general function of formative assessment in the classroom is to provide assessment-elicited evidence that informs decisions about adjusting classroom instruction. However, there are meaningful differences in certain of those definitions, and these differences sometimes affect the practices educators are adopting in the pursuit of formative assessment's instructional dividends. In Chapter 2, I offered my take on a definition:

> *Formative assessment* is a planned process in which assessment-elicited evidence of students' status is used by teachers to adjust their ongoing instructional procedures or by students to adjust their current learning tactics.

This definition, crafted in a manner to make it consonant with the findings of researchers who have studied classroom assessment, has four distinctive emphases. First, the definition stresses the need for formative assessment to be regarded as a *process* rather than a particular sort of assessment instrument. Moreover, that process is a planned one rather than a collection of a teacher's spur-of-the moment acts. Second, the formative assessment process revolves around the role played by *assessment-elicited evidence of students' status*—that is, results from formal and informal assessment procedures indicating students' current levels of achievement regarding the teacher's curricular aims. Third, the evidence garnered from such assessments is to be used by *teachers to adjust their ongoing instruction* or, fourth, by *students to adjust their current learning tactics.*

According to this definition, if any assessment results based on a district-developed assessment were relayed to a district's teachers *too late* for any resulting instructional adjustments to have a meaningful impact either on teachers' ongoing instruction or on students' current learning tactics, then this district-developed assessment would *not* be part of the formative assessment process.

We've covered quite a bit about formative assessment in this book. I noted that classroom formative assessment appears to work best when a teacher's evidence-gathering procedures are closely linked to a given curricular aim's learning progression—that is, a sequenced set of building blocks that students need to acquire en route to their mastery of a target curricular aim. I also recommended that evidence from formal or informal assessment activities be relayed to students via feedback that is skill-focused, directive, timely, and simple (Shute, 2007). I urged teachers to do their best to avoid assigning grades for their students' performances on assessments being used as part of a formative assessment process. Further, I encouraged teachers to employ frequent peer assessments and self-assessments as ways of monitoring their students' progress, because this approach optimizes students' continuing involvement in classroom formative assessment. Finally, I stressed that the way for teachers to leverage the maximum benefits of formative assessment is to regard it not as an endeavor *apart* from instruction but, rather, an integral, frequently focal element of the instructional process.

What We Know and What We Don't

As we've discussed, much of our understanding of formative assessment's potential contributions to students' learning comes from research reviews conducted by Black and Wiliam (1998a), Crooks (1988), and Kluger and Denisi (1996). It is important to understand what these reviews really tell us and what they don't. Too often these days, we see someone recommending a particular instructional procedure after invoking the "findings of an extensive research review" ostensibly supporting this recommendation. The recommender seems to expect others to instantly acquiesce because "research makes it so." Well, frequently analytic conclusions from research are simply not sufficiently corroborative. That's because, by their very nature, reviews must take into consideration a substantial range of often diverse empirical investigations and be based on a boatload of along-the-way judgments made by the researchers conducting the review.

To illustrate, when Paul Black and Dylan Wiliam carried out their widely cited review of classroom assessment research (1998a), they painstakingly analyzed 250 remarkably divergent investigations that involved students from kindergarten through college. These studies focused on a diverse range of subject areas, and featured exceedingly diverse examples of classroom formative assessment. Yet, as Black and Wiliam point out,

> The consistent feature across the variety of these examples is that they all show that attention to formative assessment can lead to significant learning gains. Although there is no guarantee that it will do so irrespective of the context and the particular approach adopted, we have not come across any report of negative effects following on an enhancement of formative practice. (1998a, pp. 11–12)

This general conclusion coincides with the one that emerged from an earlier review by Crooks (1988), namely, that formative assessment in the classroom works, big time.

Although Black and Wiliam attempted to isolate certain features of formative assessment that teachers might use to enhance students' learning, the diverse nature of the various studies reviewed meant they were unable to offer any research-sanctified suggestions about *how* formative assessment will work best in classrooms "irrespective of the context and the particular approach adopted." And, therein, we've arrived at a fundamental truth: Classroom formative assessment definitely has a positive impact on students' learning, but there is insufficient empirical evidence to tell us which particular implementations of formative assessment will work best in different instructional situations. Put another way, the manner in which the key formative assessment research reviews were carried out allowed the reviewers to generate persuasive evidence that formative assessment will improve students' learning. Moreover, these reviews give us insight into useful precepts regarding formative assessment's application. However, the manner in which these research reviews were carried out also means they can offer us few research-ratified recommendations for the specifics of how to use formative assessment in our own classrooms.

What to Do

Because classroom formative assessment benefits students, teachers ought it to use it. Still, the way a teacher employs formative assessment needs to be considered with care. Allow me to trot out three recommendations:

Recommendation 1: Approach commercial "formative assessment" materials with skepticism. Let's face it, there's a formative assessment bandwagon rolling down the road, and teachers are being called on to hop aboard. Before doing so, teachers should always try to find out more about the nature of the formative assessment approach being espoused, and determine if there's any real evidence supporting the worth of that approach.

Many of the "formative assessment procedures" teachers are being urged to adopt vary considerably in nature from the formative assessment described in relevant research reviews. For instance, Black and Wiliam (1998a) regarded classroom assessments as formative only if the use of those assessments led to actual adjustments in what was going on in class. So, if a for-profit company were trying to peddle a collection of tests as "formative assessments" but supplied no evidence that the use of those tests actually stimulated adjustments in teachers' or students' behaviors, then teachers (or the administrators making the test-adoption decision) ought to be downright doubtful about those tests' likely instructional payoffs.

Similarly, if a commercial testing firm were pressuring district administrators to buy a set of periodically administered tests described as "interim formative tests" or as "benchmark formative tests," those educators should realize that, the "formative" label notwithstanding, there's no research evidence bearing directly on the usefulness of these kinds of tests. It's not that interim or benchmark assessments are of no instructional value; they may well be useful instructional support. It's just that the positive impact of such tests has yet to be demonstrated empirically, and there is no evidence that the costs of interim tests—in terms of dollars as well as instructional time—are worth it.

Recommendation 2: Be wary of formative assessment prophets. As the instructional dividends of formative assessment become more widely known, expect to see more and more instant experts offering pay-for workshops focused on how to make formative assessment "instructionally energizing!" Again, educators need to remember that there's precious little empirical research to support the use of *particular* formative assessment procedures in *particular* contexts. So, if teachers take part in a professional development session focused on formative assessment, they should treat suggestions from the session's leader as options to be considered for possible implementation rather than as tactics that have been research sanctified. Anyone who claims there is definitive evidence that a specific incarnation of formative assessment will work in a specific setting is most definitely claiming beyond cause.

This second recommendation does not indicate the ideas put forward during such professional development activities are without merit. For instance, an insightful formative assessment workshop leader may identify a series of innovative procedures for teachers to employ during peer assessments or self-assessments, and those activities may contribute substantially to the quality of a classroom teacher's formative assessment process. If such suggestions make sense to teachers, then those suggestions should be tried out. If the suggestions work wonderfully, then teachers should keep on using them. If the suggestions don't work, then teachers should obviously dump them.

Recommendation 3: Make classroom formative assessment an integral part of instruction. This final recommendation is the most important and stems from what we know now about the likely impact of classroom formative assessment: It works, and it works well. What teachers need to find out, though, is what specific approach to formative assessment works best for them in the particular situations in which they teach. The way for teachers to approach the installation (or, possibly, the expansion) of formative assessment in their own instruction is to review some of the features identified as potential contributors to high-quality formative assessment: basing it on learning progressions, for example, and distancing it from grade giving. Next, teachers can incorporate the features they regard as most likely to be effective in their own classroom setting, then see if such procedures improve their students' learning.

For instance, let's say you're a teacher who has decided to provide students with task-focused feedback for every formative evidence-gathering procedure. Moreover, you've decided to accompany such task-focused feedback with at least two suggestions for each student's additional or alternative study. After using this approach for a few weeks, you reflect on how it's working and decide whether to make it a routine part of your own formative assessment procedures. The underlying idea, of course, is that teachers will ultimately arrive at a combination of formative assessment tactics that work just right for them, just right for what they're teaching, and just right for the students they teach.

At the close of Chapter 5, I explained that formative assessment can actually be conceptualized as four separate levels: (1) teachers' instructional adjustments, (2) students' learning tactic adjustments, (3) a classroom climate change, and (4) schoolwide implementation. Teachers may, of course, choose to work only at Level 1 formative assessment with its focus on a teacher's making adjustments in instruction. But if a teacher decides to take a swing at Level 2 or Level 3 formative assessment, there will be plenty of opportunities for the teacher to try out different approaches and see "what happens if?"

Overridingly, teachers need to regard classroom formative assessment procedures not as something separate from their instruction but, instead, as a necessary dimension of how they teach. If teachers decide to accept this third recommendation, their resultant reliance on evidence gathering for instructional adjustments should, in time, make formative assessment almost indistinguishable from teaching. Quite literally, teachers simply won't be able to think about their instructional decision making without regarding formative assessment as an indispensable part of that process. Well-designed instruction is likely to be successful. Well-designed instruction accompanied by formative assessment is almost certain to be successful.

The Impact of Educational Accountability

Test-based educational accountability has come to exert an enormous impact on what transpires in classrooms. Some of the resultant classroom changes have been beneficial—that is, they have improved students' learning. Many of those classroom changes have been harmful—that is, they have decreased or distorted students' learning.

What We Know and What We Don't

Teachers know for sure just how much personal pressure they experience as a consequence of whatever accountability system affects their schools. Some teachers' students are assessed each year, and those students' performances are regarded as the chief indicator of an individual teacher's instructional prowess. Other teachers don't have to run the personal accountability-testing gauntlet themselves but still find their school's overall perceived effectiveness dependent on how well other teachers' students perform on each year's accountability tests. If you are a teacher whose *school's* students flop on annual accountability tests, even though you've had no specific responsibility for teaching those students, you'll still be a faculty member in a "failing" school. Just like success, failure rubs off on folks.

Depending on the particulars of any accountability system in which a teacher functions, the impact of educational accountability on that teacher's own instruction might be modest or major. We've all seen reports about accountability systems that appear to have led to improved student achievement and to reductions in the persistent gaps between performances of minority and majority students (Center on Education Policy, 2007). Yet, we also know that ill-conceived accountability systems can surely cause educational harm.

Ample experience shows us that pressure to boost students' scores on accountability tests can lead to *curricular reductionism* whereby curricular content thought unlikely to be tested is simply removed from a teacher's instructional plate. Sometimes teachers do this sort of curricular winnowing themselves; in other instances, site-based administrators, district administrators, or state administrators limit the curriculum to test-eligible content. Regardless of who makes the cuts, the consequence is identical: Students end up not learning some of the things they ought to be learning.

Regrettably, we have also seen the rise of *excessive test-preparation* activities that eat up instructional time and turn classrooms into joyless drill factories. Sometimes excessive test-prep is initiated by teachers, and sometimes it's forced on teachers by school administrators or district administrators. Given the enormous pressure on teachers and administrators, as well as the significant consequences of low test scores, this practice is surely understandable. But it's still unacceptable.

Finally, we have seen too many instances of *modeled dishonesty*, in which teachers or administrators engage in blatantly improper test preparation, test-administration, or test-scoring conduct. Although, again, we can understand why accountability-buffeted administrators or teachers might cheat in an effort to raise students' test scores, such behavior sends a deplorable message to students. When adults model misconduct for children, the ensuing damage can be irreparable.

So we know that poorly conceptualized educational accountability programs can lead to all sorts of instructional absurdities. But this does not make educational accountability programs inherently evil. Citizens who pay for tax-supported schools have a right to hold educators accountable. Parents who send their children to those tax-supported schools have a right to expect their children to be well taught.

What most educators don't know is how best to fix a broken educational accountability program. That's what we'll look into next.

What to Do

Complaining is the easy thing. It's much simpler to complain about an unacceptable situation than it is to try to improve it. But an unacceptable educational accountability system is almost certain to have an adverse impact on the quality of a teacher's instruction. And adversely impacted instruction surely shortchanges students. So, easy or not, teachers must attempt to remedy any accountability system that's having a negative effect on their teaching.

Whether educators decide to undertake such remedy-focused actions on their own or in collaboration with others (perhaps as part of a professional association), what's most important is that educators *at least try* to alter accountability-induced circumstances that appear to be harming students. Here, then, are two closely related recommendations on how to modify an educational accountability program so it becomes more kid-helpful than kid-harmful.

Recommendation 1: If an accountability program's tests are instructionally insensitive, take appropriate action. Teachers who are fortunate enough to find themselves teaching in a system where the accountability test is instructionally sensitive have much to be happy about. Yet, even well-designed accountability systems can be fine-tuned to ensure tests have a beneficial rather than detrimental effect on students' learning. If educators, solo or with allies, offer practical suggestions to authorities about how to improve the instructional consequences of an existing accountability test, it's just possible that those suggestions might be accepted.

More often than not, however, educators will find themselves in a situation where the backbone of an accountability system is a set of tests that are instructionally *insensitive*. As you saw, my recommendation is for these educators to "take appropriate action." However, what sorts of action would be "appropriate"?

Action 1: Lobby for test replacement. The first type of appropriate action is for these educators to try their best to get the accountability program's instructionally insensitive tests replaced by instructionally sensitive ones. As we discussed in Chapter 2, the two most common types of instructionally insensitive tests are (1) traditional, standardized achievement tests based on a comparative assessment approach and (2) certain kinds of standards-based accountability tests. The case to be made for instructionally sensitive assessment in an accountability program begins with the fact these tests offer the chief way to accurately determine a school's success. Beyond the valid evaluative data instructionally *sensitive* tests generate, they can serve as a catalyst for better teaching. For an accountability system to have a beneficial impact on teachers' instruction, that system needs to focus on exactly this dual mission: accurate accountability decisions *and* the promotion of improved classroom instruction.

Action 2: Go public. Despite educators' valiant efforts to have instructionally insensitive accountability tests replaced by instructionally sensitive ones, such a change often just won't take place. Accordingly, the second type of "appropriate action" educators can take is to help initiate a major public information campaign about the nature of appropriate-versus-inappropriate accountability tests. That is, educators can set out to educate relevant constituencies about the perils of trying to evaluate instructional effectiveness when using the wrong kinds of accountability tests. These "relevant constituencies," of course, vary from setting to setting. For one group of educators, it might be just the parents of the students they teach. Another group of educators might target their educative efforts to all local citizens, with a special focus on influential decision makers, such as school board members. Educators even might try to bring these sorts of assessment issues to the attention of local or national legislators.

The essence of the message these educators are trying to convey is simple: *The wrong kinds of accountability tests are supplying inaccurate evaluations of our schools.* Because such tests mask the quality of teaching going on there, they are actually having a detrimental effect: making it impossible to tell when an instructor is effective and when an instructor is ineffective. A follow-up corollary to that message is that it is possible to *replace* the wrong kind of accountability tests (instructionally insensitive ones) with the right kind of accountability tests (instructionally sensitive ones). These efforts have the best odds of success when the educators who conduct them address accountability head-on and communicate directly that they are not hiding from accountability but, rather, advocating on behalf of children.

I have argued elsewhere (Popham, 2001) that one of the most effective strategies for educators looking to replace inappropriate accountability tests with appropriate ones is to engage in a two-step operation. It commences with (1) a parent education effort and is followed by (2) a disaffiliation from such parents. The way this approach would work is for educators to supply parents with sufficient doses of *assessment literacy* so that those parents understand clearly why it is that certain kinds of ill-conceived accountability programs, particularly those that incorporate instructionally insensitive tests, end up distorting education and, as a consequence, *harming those parents' children.*

Once educators believe that a group of parents is sufficiently knowledgeable about the shortcomings of existing accountability tests, those educators can outline various ways a nonpartisan parent group might bring about sufficient pressure on elected policymakers to remedy the situation. Materials could be supplied to such parent groups that succinctly identify weaknesses in the current accountability tests and suggest the kinds of tests that should be used as replacements. At that point, however, all educators should withdraw from these groups. If parent groups are going to act, they should do so on their own. Nonpartisan groups, unaffiliated in any way with educators, can exercise far more political punch on this issue than can any organizational alliances involving educators.

Recommendation 2: Enhance your own assessment literacy. This second recommendation is also related to the instructional impact of external accountability tests but in a way that's more general than specific. It may seem strange to find a book about instruction concluding with a recommendation that educators beef up their knowledge about educational assessment. After all, most teachers went into the field of education to teach, not to test. But, as I have reiterated often in these pages, educational measurement has changed today's instructional game. Testing has become a pivotal part of what teachers do and how teachers are judged. And this is why all educators, teachers and administrators, need to advance their assessment literacy.

This is a mission educators can embark on solo or in concert with colleagues. On a solo basis, of course, an educator can dig into any of the materials described in the Suggestions for Further Reading throughout this book. For many, solitary learning is a preferred way to acquire new skills and knowledge. However, the use of professional learning communities (PLCs) will typically make a quest for assessment literacy more successful (McLaughlin & Talbert, 2006; Wald & Castleberry, 2000). When several educators read the same jointly chosen materials, then periodically interact with one another to discuss the issues raised in those materials, the ensuing depth of assessment literacy is likely to be more appropriate for all concerned.

Formal professional development courses on assessment are also an option, particularly if such courses can be deliberately fashioned to deal with the instructionally relevant information about assessment that today's educators need. Measurement courses offered by colleges and universities represent another potential route by which educators can acquire sufficient assessment literacy. Just be certain such courses have a *practical* bent. If educators discover their local colleges and universities are dishing out assessment courses beclouded in psychometric esoterica rather than focused on real-world instruction, it's time to petition the institution's officers to update their offerings.

Whatever the source, and with or without colleagues, this final recommendation is one that can have a profound effect on the way an educator functions. Educators will find myriad occasions, day in and day out, when their heightened knowledge of measurement will lead to better educational decisions. And, of course, better educational decisions will contribute to students' improved education.

The Final Wrap-Up

In retrospect, this book about teaching has focused on how to make a teacher's instruction more successful. Many topics were treated, but don't let all those topics deflect you from recognizing that a teacher's key instructional decisions will always fall into four fundamental categories: (1) curriculum determination, (2) instructional design, (3) instructional monitoring, and (4) instructional evaluation. The decisions teachers make in each of those four stages will determine how successful their instruction will be.

Teaching is a complicated endeavor. Anyone who's taught for more than 15 minutes will agree. The best way to navigate that complexity is to reduce instruction to its essentials. Teachers begin by identifying a set of curricular aims they want their students to achieve. Teachers then design a set of instructional activities they think will help students achieve those aims. As those activities are taking place, teachers monitor how well their instruction is working and, if necessary, adjust the instruction. Finally, to find out if their instruction worked, teachers determine if students' post-instruction performances indicate that the intended curricular aims have been accomplished. Successful instructional designs can, with few modifications, be offered again to future students. Unsuccessful instructional approaches, of course, should be revamped, sometimes substantially, before being used again with other students.

As I've stressed throughout this book, teaching is also an ends-means undertaking. The more clearheaded teachers are about the curricular ends their instruction is supposed to accomplish, the more likely it is that that those teachers' along-the-way instructional decisions will be clearheaded. And, incontestably, clearheaded instructional decisions will help students learn what they're supposed to learn.

Finally, today's teachers are further challenged to carry out their work in an unprecedented age of educational accountability. Pressured by constant demands for hard evidence that instruction has been successful, many teachers feel their skills are now under relentless scrutiny. As they are painfully aware, it's a case of measure up or be seen as an instructional failure. But the first step in being able to measure up instructionally is to avoid becoming overwhelmed by accountability-induced anxieties. What teachers must do instead is give thoughtful attention to curriculum choices, and then to the design, monitoring, and evaluation of instruction. As much as education has changed over the years, those four sets of decisions are what good teaching has always been about. They still are.

✔ Chapter Check-Back

- Research reviews indicate that classroom formative assessments can markedly enhance students' learning, but these reviews do not tell us definitively which formative assessment techniques work the best in any particular setting.
- Educators should approach formative assessment claims and products from commercial organizations with skepticism, be wary of formative assessment evangelists, and adopt formative assessment as an integral part of instruction.
- Educators should work to eliminate instructionally insensitive tests from accountability programs and to enhance their personal assessment literacy.
- Despite teaching's inherent complexity, it is fundamentally an ends-means undertaking in which teachers engage in curriculum determination, instructional design, instructional monitoring, and instructional evaluation.

Suggestions for Further Reading

Criswell, J. R. (2006). *Developing assessment literacy: A guide for elementary and middle school teachers.* Norwood, MA: Christopher-Gordon.

Criswell presents a powerful argument that teachers desperately need to attain a reasonable degree of assessment literacy and then identifies the chief content that he regards as being requisite for classroom teachers to master. Although written for elementary and middle school teachers, the book also has much relevance to the concerns of high school teachers.

Popham, W. J. (2001). *The truth about testing: An educator's call to action.* Alexandria, VA: ASCD.

Here, you'll find ways of distinguishing between sound and unsound accountability tests, guidelines for maximizing the instructional yield of classroom assessments, and evidence-gathering strategies to buttress results of external accountability exams. The book concludes with an array of action-options for educators who wish to install instructionally supportive accountability tests.

Popham, W. J. (2006). *Mastering assessment: A self-service system for educators.* New York: Routledge.

This collection of 15 booklets, each pertaining to a separate assessment-related topic, was designed for use as part of a school's professional development program focused on the function of assessment literacy.

Popham, W. J. (2009). *Unlearned lessons: Six stumbling blocks to our schools' success.* Cambridge, MA: Harvard Education Press.

This book identifies six serious mistakes educators have made during the past half-century and argues that our failure to learn from these lessons has seriously diminished the quality of schooling. Suggestions are offered for resolving each of these six shortcomings.

Resources

Black, P., & Wiliam, D. (1998a). Assessment and classroom learning. *Assessment in Education, 5*(1), 7–74.

Black, P., & Wiliam, D. (1998b). Raising standards through classroom assessment. *Phi Delta Kappan, 80*(2), 139–148.

Black, P., Harrison C., Lee, C., Marshall, B., & Wiliam, D. (2004). Working inside the black box: Assessment for learning in the classroom. *Phi Delta Kappan, 86*(1), 8–21.

Center on Education Policy. (2007, May 31). *Answering the question that matters most: Has student achievement increased since No Child Left Behind?* Washington, DC: Author. Available: www.cep-dc.org

Council of Chief State School Officers. (2006). *Formative assessment and CCSSO: A special initiative, a special opportunity.* Washington, DC: Author.

Crooks, T. J. (1988). The impact of classroom evaluation on students. *Review of Educational Research, 58*(4), 438–481.

Kluger, A. N., & Denisi, A. (1996). The effects of feedback interventions on performance: A historical review, a meta-analysis, and a preliminary feedback intervention theory. *Psychological Bulletin, 119*(2), 254–284.

Leahy, S., Lyon, C., Thompson, M., & Wiliam, D. (2005, November). Classroom assessment—Minute by minute, day by day. *Educational Leadership, 63*(3), 18–24.

Likert, R. (1932). A technique for the measurement of attitudes. *Archives of Psychology,* 140.

Marzano, R. J. (2007). *The art and science of teaching: A comprehensive framework for effective teaching.* Alexandria, VA: ASCD.

Marzano, R. J., Pickering, D. J., & Pollock, J. E. (2001). *Classroom instruction that works: Research-based strategies for increasing student achievement.* Alexandria, VA: ASCD.

Masters, G., & Forster, M. (1996). *Progress maps.* Melbourne: Australian Council on Educational Research.

McLaughlin, M., & Talbert, J. E. (2006). *Building school-based teacher learning communities: Professional strategies to improve student achievement.* New York: Teachers College Press.

Popham, W. J. (1988). Judgment-based teacher evaluation. In S. J. Stanley & W. J. Popham (Eds.), *Teacher evaluation: Six prescriptions for success* (pp. 56–77). Alexandria, VA: ASCD.

Popham, W. J. (2001). *The truth about testing: An educator's call to action.* Alexandria, VA: ASCD.

Popham, W. J. (2008). *Transformative assessment.* Alexandria, VA: ASCD.

Scriven, M. (1967). The methodology of evaluation. In R. W. Tyler, R. M. Gagné, & M. Scriven (Eds.), *Perspectives of curriculum evaluation* (pp. 39–83). Chicago: Rand McNally.

Shute, V. J. (2007). *Focus on formative feedback* (ETS Research Report No. RR-07-26). Princeton, NJ: Education Testing Service.

Tomlinson, C. A. (2001). *How to differentiate instruction in mixed-ability classrooms* (2nd ed.). Alexandria, VA: ASCD

Wald, P. J., & Castleberry, M. S. (2000). *Educators as learners: Creating a professional learning community in your school.* Alexandria, VA: ASCD.

Wiggins, G., & McTighe, J. (2005). *Understanding by design* (2nd ed.). Alexandria, VA: ASCD.

Wiliam, D. (2007). Keeping learning on track: Classroom assessment and the regulation of learning. In F. K. Lester, Jr. (Ed.), *Second handbook of mathematics teaching and learning* (pp. 1053–1098). Greenwich, CT: Information Age Publishing.

Wiliam, D., & Thompson, M. (2008). Integrating assessment with instruction: What will it take to make it work? In C. A. Dwyer (Ed.), *The future of assessment: Shaping teaching and learning.* Mahwah, NJ: Lawrence Erlbaum Associates.

Index

The letter *f* following a page number denotes a figure.

About the Author

 **W. James Popham** is Emeritus Professor in the UCLA Graduate School of Education and Information Studies. He has spent most of career as a teacher, largely at UCLA, where for nearly 30 years he taught courses in instructional methods for prospective teachers and graduate-level courses in evaluation and measurement. At UCLA he won several distinguished teaching awards, and in January 2000, he was recognized by *UCLA Today* as one of UCLA's top 20 professors of the 20th century.

In 1968, Dr. Popham established IOX Assessment Associates, a research and development group that created statewide student achievement tests for a dozen states. In 2002 the National Council on Measurement in Education presented him with its Award for Career Contributions to Educational Measurement. He is a former president of the American Educational Research Association (AERA) and the founding editor of *Educational Evaluation and Policy Analysis,* AERA's quarterly journal. In 2006 he was awarded a Certificate of Recognition by the National Association of Test Directors.

Dr. Popham is the author of more than 20 books, 200 journal articles, 50 research reports, and nearly 200 papers presented before research societies. His most recent books are *Unlearned Lessons: Six Stumbling Blocks to Our Schools' Success* (2009), *Transformative Assessment* (2008), *Classroom Assessment: What Teachers Need to Know, 5th Ed.* (2008); *Assessment for Educational Leaders* (2006); *Mastering Assessment: A Self-Service System for Educators* (2006); *America's "Failing" Schools: How Parents and Teachers Can Cope with No Child Left Behind* (2005); *Test Better, Teach Better: The Instructional Role of Assessment* (2003); and *The Truth About Testing: An Educator's Call to Action* (2001).

Related ASCD Resources: Assessment and Instruction

At the time of publication, the following ASCD resources were available; for the most up-to-date information about ASCD resources, go to www.ascd.org. ASCD stock numbers are noted in parentheses.

Mixed Media
Balanced Assessment: Enhancing Learning with Evidence-Centered Teaching: An ASCD Professional Inquiry Kit (eight activity folders and a CD-ROM) by Joseph Ciofala, ETS (#905057)

Print Products
The Art and Science of Teaching: A Comprehensive Framework for Effective Instruction by Robert J. Marzano (#107001)
Changing the Way You Teach, Improving the Way Students Learn by Giselle Martin-Kniep and Joanne Picone-Zocchia (#108001)
Checking for Understanding: Formative Assessment Techniques for Your Classroom by Douglas Fisher and Nancy Frey (#107023)
Classroom Instruction That Works: Research Based Strategies for Increasing Student Achievement by Robert J. Marzano, Debra J. Pickering, and Jane E. Pollock (#101010)
Transformative Assessment by W. James Popham (#108018)

Video
The Art and Science of Teaching Video Series (two 45-minute DVDs with an embedded PowerPoint presentation and teacher handouts) (#608074)
The Power of Formative Assessment (three DVDs with a user's guide) (#608066) Also available as individual programs, each with a user's guide: Increasing Motivation and Achievement (#608067); *A Six-Step Process for Student Growth* (#608068); and *Strategies for Checking for Understanding* (#608069)

For additional resources, visit us on the World Wide Web (http://www.ascd.org), send an e-mail message to member@ascd.org, call the ASCD Service Center (1-800-933-ASCD or 703-578-9600, then press 2), send a fax to 703-575-5400, or write to Information Services, ASCD, 1703 N. Beauregard St., Alexandria, VA 22311-1714 USA.